Aging Honorably and Happily

Frank R. Shivers

LIGHTNING SOURCE
1246 Heil Quaker Blvd,
La Vergne, TN

Unless otherwise noted, Scripture quotations are from
The Holy Bible *King James Version*

Library of Congress Cataloging-in-Publication Data

Shivers, Frank R., 1949-
Aging Honorably and Happily / Frank Shivers
ISBN 978-1-878127-26-8

Library of Congress Control Number:
2017911071

Cover design by
Tim King of Click Graphics, Inc.

For Information:
Frank Shivers Evangelistic Association
P. O. Box 9991
Columbia, South Carolina 29290
www.frankshivers.com

Presented to

_____

By

_____

Date

_____

It is autumn; not without
But within me is the cold.
Youth and spring are all about;
It is I that have grown old.[1]

~ Henry Wadsworth Longfellow

I'm growing fonder of my staff;
I'm growing dimmer in my eyes;
I'm growing fainter in my laugh;
I'm growing deeper in my sighs;
I'm growing careless of my dress;
I'm growing frugal of my gold;
I'm growing wise; I'm growing...yes,
I'm growing old.

I see it in my changing taste;
I see it in my changing hair;
I see it in my growing waist;
I see it in my growing heir;
A thousand signs proclaim the truth,
As plain as truth was ever told,
That, even in my vaunted youth,
I'm growing old![2]

~ John Godfrey Saxe

God declares that He is not simply the God of the young saint, that He is not simply the God of the middle-aged saint, but that He is the God of the saints in all their ages from the cradle to the tomb....God himself is the same, whatever may be our age; and... God's dealings towards us, both in providence and in grace, His carryings and His deliverings, are alike unchanged.[3]

~ C. H. Spurgeon

To

Dr. Billy Graham
Thank you, Billy, for impacting my life as a teenager through your sermons and service to our Lord, picturing to me what a biblical evangelist "looked" like. Doubtlessly the Lord used both to prepare me for the call to vocational evangelism and its task nearly fifty years ago.

You have faithfully revealed by life and lip how to run the Christian race. And now in the season of "old age" you are demonstrating how to finish it well.

In behalf of the millions (including me) your ministry has impacted yesterday and today, I say thank you for having fought the good fight, having finished the race, and having remained faithful.

Whoever first said it was right—growing old is not for sissies.[4]

~ Billy Graham

Contents

Preface

Death and taxes are inevitable. But so also is old age if we live long enough. It is therefore prudent to give the "golden years" thought and preparation if you are upon their brink and consideration in living them to the fullest for the glory of God if you are already in their midst. Biblical insight as to how best to grow older gracefully, honorably and happily is for all.

God wants us to remember that life is short (James 4:14); that the beauty of youth is soon gone (Proverbs 31:30; 1 Peter 1:24); that all of life has its purpose (Psalm 92:12–14); that He will sustain His children in old age (Ruth 4:15) and that growing old is honorable (Proverbs 16:31; 20:29). As His replicas, God wants the elderly to know that they "retain their value as persons whose contributions to all generations should not be ignored."[5]

Billy Graham voiced the experience of many when he stated, "All my life I've been taught how to die, but no one ever taught me how to grow old."[6] Odds are that the same is true with you. *Aging Honorably and Happily* teaches one how to grow old spiritually, emotionally and physically.

Included with each chapter are two or three jokes to bring a chuckle and smile (*Just for Laughs*). Solomon states that "a merry heart doeth good like a medicine" (Proverbs 17:22). These jokes certainly will be the most enjoyable, if not the most beneficial, medicine on the nightstand.

The thing that may be wrong with the book is that I may be too young to write it. I am, after all, only sixty-eight. No doubt a better job could have been done had I waited until I was a hundred years old to write it. By the way, I do reserve the right to revise this edition then!

They say there are three stages of old age: the young-old (approximately 65–74), the middle-old (ages 75–84), and the old-

Aging Honorably and Happily

old (over age 85)—or humorously but perhaps truthfully put, the Go-Go years, the Slow-Go years, and the No-Go years. In whichever stage this book finds you, it is my prayer that it will only be bettered, happier and healthier for having read its pages.

From the pen of the tremendous and incredible missionary to China Dr. C. T. Studd comes a fitting challenge for the living of all of life, especially its last part.

Only One Life

Two little lines I heard one day,
Traveling along life's busy way,
Bringing conviction to my heart
And from my mind would not depart:
Only one life, 'twill soon be past;
Only what's done for Christ will last.

Only one life, yes only one,
Soon will its fleeting hours be done,
Then in that day my Lord to meet
And stand before His Judgement seat.
Only one life, 'twill soon be past;
Only what's done for Christ will last.

Only one life, the still small voice
Gently pleads for a better choice,
Bidding me selfish aims to leave
And to God's holy will to cleave.
Only one life, 'twill soon be past;
Only what's done for Christ will last.

Only one life, a few brief years,
Each with its burdens, hopes, and fears;
Each with its clays I must fulfill,

Preface

Living for self or in His will.
Only one life, 'twill soon be past;
Only what's done for Christ will last.

When this bright world would tempt me sore,
When Satan would a victory score,
When self would seek to have its way,
Then help me Lord with joy to say,
"Only one life, 'twill soon be past;
Only what's done for Christ will last."

Give me, Father, a purpose deep
In joy or sorrow Thy Word to keep,
Faithful and true what e'er the strife,
Pleasing Thee in my daily life.
Only one life, 'twill soon be past;
Only what's done for Christ will last.

Oh, let my love with fervor burn;
And from the world now let me turn,
Living for Thee and Thee alone,
Bringing Thee pleasure on Thy throne.
Only one life, 'twill soon be past;
Only what's done for Christ will last.

Only one life, yes only one,
Now let me say, "Thy will be done";
And when at last I'll hear the call,
I know I'll say, "'Twas worth it all."
Only one life, 'twill soon be past;
Only what's done for Christ will last.

"LORD, remind me how brief my time on earth will be. Remind me that my days are numbered—how fleeting my life is" (Psalm 39:4 NLT).

The Lord is my light and my salvation; whom shall I fear? the Lord is the strength of my life; of whom shall I be afraid?

~ Psalm 27:1

But the spirit of fear is not harmless; it's deeply damaging, destructive, and debilitating. The Bible speaks of "the bondage of fear."[7] ~ Adrian Rogers

Fear is a great masquerader. What scares you can be scared off. Everything that scares you can be scared off by God. Let fear push you Godward.[8] ~ Dick Lincoln

Lurking in the shadows around every imaginable corner, [fear] threatens to poison your inner peace and outward poise. Bully that it is, the creature relies on scare tactics and surprise attacks.[9] ~ Chuck Swindoll

What lies behind us and what lies before us are tiny matters compared to what lies within us. ~ Ralph Waldo Emerson

1

Kiss Away the Fear

Elisabeth Elliot was asked how a person could look toward the aging process with anticipation instead of dread and fear. She answered that for her it was possible by looking at old age as the vestibule of Heaven and knowing that God was bearing her as a lamb in His bosom. [10] Elliot said that she thought often about the hymn "How Firm a Foundation."

E'en down to old age all My people shall prove
My boundless, eternal, unchangeable love;
And then when gray hairs shall their temples adorn,
Like lambs they shall still in My bosom be borne.

The banishment of fear in old age involves accepting rather than rejecting the aging process based upon knowledge that God sovereignly is in control of our lives and is trustworthy.

Robert Browning underscores this truth in saying,

Grow old along with me!
The best is yet to be, the last of life,
    for which the first was made.
Our times are in His hand who saith,
"A whole I planned; youth shows but half.
    Trust God; see all, nor be afraid!"

Paul declared, "For which cause we faint not; but though our outward man perish, yet the inward man is renewed day by day. For our light affliction, which is but for a moment, worketh for us a far more exceeding and eternal weight of glory; while we look not at the things which are seen, but at the things which are not seen: for the things which are seen are temporal; but the things which are not seen are eternal" (2 Corinthians 4:16–18).

Aging Honorably and Happily

Dr. William Barclay in his commentary on this text states why the believer need not fear aging. He says, "All through life it must happen that a man's bodily strength fades away, but all through life it ought to happen that a man's soul keeps growing. From the physical point of view life may be a slow but inevitable slipping down the slope that leads to death. But from the spiritual point of view life is a climbing up the hill that leads to the presence of God. No man need fear the years, for they bring him nearer, not to death, but to God."[11]

Perhaps you recall that as a child when you scraped a knee or arm your mother would "kiss away the hurt." Well, the great London pastor of the nineteenth century C. H. Spurgeon says that God "kisses away" the fear of aging with His promises. These promises include:

Philippians 1:6 (AMPC): "And I am convinced *and* sure of this very thing, that He Who began a good work in you will continue until the day of Jesus Christ [right up to the time of His return], developing [that good work] *and* perfecting *and* bringing it to full completion in you."

Romans 8:37–39 (NLT): "No, despite all these things, over-whelming victory is ours through Christ, who loved us. And I am convinced that nothing can ever separate us from God's love. Neither death nor life, neither angels nor demons, neither our fears for today nor our worries about tomorrow—not even the powers of hell can separate us from God's love. No power in the sky above or in the earth below—indeed, nothing in all creation will ever be able to separate us from the love of God that is revealed in Christ Jesus our Lord."

Psalm 84:11: "For the LORD God is a sun and shield: the LORD will give grace and glory: no good thing will he withhold from them that walk uprightly."

Kiss Away the Fear

Isaiah 46:4 (NASB): "Even to *your* old age I will be the same, and even to *your* graying years I will bear *you*! I have done *it*, and I will carry *you*; and I will bear *you* and I will deliver *you*."

Jude 24 (NIV): "[He] is able to keep you from stumbling and to present you before his glorious presence without fault and with great joy."

Romans 8:31: "What shall we then say to these things? If God be for us, who can be against us?"

Psalm 46:1–3: "God is our refuge and strength, a very present help in trouble. Therefore will not we fear, though the earth be removed, and though the mountains be carried into the midst of the sea; Though the waters thereof roar and be troubled, though the mountains shake with the swelling thereof."

Job 5:26 (NET): "You will come to your grave in a full age, As stacks of grain are harvested in their season."

Standing on the promises of Christ my King,
    Through eternal ages let His praises ring;
"Glory in the highest," I will shout and sing,
    Standing on the promises of God.

Standing on the promises that cannot fail;
    When the howling storms of doubt and fear assail,
By the living Word of God I shall prevail,
    Standing on the promises of God.

Standing on the promises of Christ the Lord,
    Bound to him eternally by love's strong cord,
Overcoming daily with the Spirit's sword,
    Standing on the promises of God.

Standing on the promises I cannot fall,
    Listening every moment to the Spirit's call,

Aging Honorably and Happily

Resting in my Savior as my all in all,
    Standing on the promises of God. ~ Russell Kelso Carter

View each promise as a kiss from God that calms your fear, and you will discover with the multitudes in old age that they are an effective antitoxin.

Just for Laughs

In the school play a little boy had a part that read, "It is I; be not afraid." He came out on the stage and said, "It is me and I'm scared."[12]

A young man got a job in a potato factory which simply entailed the separation of various size potatoes. After several days the boy informed the boss that he was quitting due to the difficulty of the job. The boss didn't understand. He said, "All I asked you to do is to separate the small, medium and large potatoes from one another."

The boy replied, "I know. But I got tired of making all those decisions."

Bob Hope said, "You know you're old when the candles cost more than the cake."

It is just in proportion as we live upon Him that we are strong Christians. To live on Christ, to draw all from Christ, to do all in the strength of Christ, to ever be looking to Christ; this is the true secret of spiritual prosperity.[13] ~ J. C. Ryle

God grant that I may never live to be useless.[14] ~ John Wesley

So few finish well—really well.[15] ~ Charles Swindoll

I do hope my Father will let the river of my life go flowing fully until the finish. I don't want it to end in a swamp.[16]
~ F. B. Meyer

Bring me my bow of burning gold;
   Bring me my arrows of desire.
Bring me my spear; oh, clouds unfold!
   Bring me my chariot of fire!

We shall not cease from battle strife,
   Nor shall the sword sleep in our hand,
Till we have built Jerusalem
   In this fair and pleasant land. ~ William Blake, "And Did Those Feet in Ancient Time" (adapted)

2

Finish Strong—Finish Well

Dr. J. Robert Clinton, professor of leadership at Fuller Theological Seminary, spent fifteen years researching the development of around one thousand leaders (Old Testament patriarchs, priests, military leaders; New Testament apostles, prophets, evangelists, teachers and pastors). Data was available on only forty-nine to analyze how they finished. Clinton's finding shockingly was that only thirty percent of these finished well. As we grow older, may it be our determination not to falter as seventy percent of these forty-nine Bible leaders did but to finish strong and well.[17]

In his book *Running and Being,* George Sheehan writes, "I am at my best nearing the finish of a race. Until then I am just another mediocre distance runner, just one of the many run-of-the-mill competitors well back in the pack. But with the finish line in sight, all that changes. Now I am the equal of anyone—gray-haired, balding and wrinkled, but world class. Gasping, wheezing and groaning, but unbeatable."[18] Sheehan battled cancer and died. He ran life's race and finished strong.

As with Dr. Sheehan, the day will arrive for us to finish life's race. As we think of finishing the course of life well and strong, there is no better example to consider than that of the Apostle Paul. As he sat in a Roman prison, anticipating an imminent death, he wrote to Timothy:

2 Timothy 4:6–8 (ESV): "For I am already being poured out as a drink offering, and the time of my departure has come. I have fought the good fight, I have finished the race, I have kept the faith. Henceforth there is laid up for me the crown of righteousness, which the Lord, the righteous judge, will award to me on that Day, and not only to me but also to all who have loved his appearing."

Aging Honorably and Happily

The word "departure" *(analusis)* is a nautical term used to describe a ship lifting anchor and setting sail, an army breaking camp to move out, and a person being freed from his chains. Using this picturesque term, Paul cites his forthcoming death. He soon will pull up anchor and set sail, break camp with the world and be freed from the cares and trials of this life to go Home. And he says that day will be met without regret, for he has fought a good fight, finished the race and kept the faith.

Paul sums up his life in three ways. He states, "I have fought a good fight." When an athlete can really say that he has done his best in a contest, then there is great satisfaction in his heart whether he wins or loses.[19] At the end of his life, Paul now looks back without regret knowing he gave it his best shot.

Upon his mother's death, Barrie said, "I can look back and I cannot see the smallest thing undone."[20] Knowledge that we have done our best produces satisfaction like nothing else.

Live your life to the end, knowing that you rolled up your sleeves and fought every round for God and against Satan to the best of your ability.

Paul next states, "I have finished the course." It is one thing to start a race, another to finish it. A famous man refused to allow a biography of his life to be written while he was yet alive. In defense of the decision he said, "I have seen so many men fall out on the last lap."[21]

It has been many years now that I have prayed, "Lord, take me home before dark." I want to finish well and strong. I certainly don't want to fall out on the last lap. I know that if I'm incautious I can spoil and damage a lifetime of service and godly reputation in a moment's time. All can.

Paul was finishing the race victoriously. However, to his sorrow one of his counterparts faltered in the race. Writing of

Finish Strong—Finish Well

Demas, Paul says, "Demas, in love with this present world, has deserted me and gone to Thessalonica" (2 Timothy 4:10 NIV). Demas anticipated finishing the race well as Paul his mentor had, but the stuff of the present world tripped him up.

You and I could wind up as Demas if we are not careful. Like Paul, come what may, let's finish the race well. It's always too soon to quit.

In the third place he states, "I have kept the faith." That is, he maintained doctrinal integrity with regard to the Holy Scriptures and retained to the end confidence in the fact that Jesus Christ was his Savior and Lord, despite the opposition and persecution experienced.

It wasn't an easy road he traveled. In 2 Corinthians 11:23–27 (The Message), Paul recalls some of the trials and conflicts that he experienced.

"I've worked much harder, been jailed more often, beaten up more times than I can count, and at death's door time after time. I've been flogged five times with the Jews' thirty-nine lashes, beaten by Roman rods three times, pummeled with rocks once. I've been shipwrecked three times, and immersed in the open sea for a night and a day. In hard traveling year in and year out, I've had to ford rivers, fend off robbers, struggle with friends, struggle with foes. I've been at risk in the city, at risk in the country, endangered by desert sun and sea storm, and betrayed by those I thought were my brothers. I've known drudgery and hard labor, many a long and lonely night without sleep, many a missed meal, blasted by the cold, naked to the weather."

Yet after enduring all of that Paul says, "I have kept the faith." God grant us grace and grit to keep the faith to the end regardless of the hardship, heartache, hostility and hurt.

At the 1968 Olympics, an hour after the marathon's winner

crossed the finish line Tanzania's John Stephen Akhwari limped across the finish line, having been injured in a fall early in the race. Upon being asked why he didn't quit, he said, "My country did not send me 7,000 miles to start this race. My country sent me to finish." God didn't simply send you to start the race but to finish it well like Paul did, regardless of the difficulty incurred in its running. Determine you're in it to finish it and to finish it well.

Finishing Well Is No Accident

To finish life well requires that we "be strong in the Lord and in His mighty power" (Ephesians 6:10 NIV). How? The Bible scholar Matthew Henry states, "We have no sufficient strength of our own. Our natural courage is as perfect cowardice and our natural strength as perfect weakness, but all our sufficiency is of God. In His strength we must go forth and go on."[22]

Henry in that one sentence summarizes the single most important thing necessary for us to finish the race of life strong and well. It is a constant awareness of our utter spiritual weakness in battling Satan and utmost reliance upon Jesus Christ for strength and mighty power. "In His strength we must go forth and go on."[23] Jesus Christ alone can give the victory over the evil one because of His triumph over him through His crucifixion and resurrection. Let us appropriate that power through faith (Philippians 3:10; Galatians 2:20).

Put on the Armor of God

After exhorting the believer to be strong spiritually, Paul instructs him to dress for warfare daily (6:10–18). The armor that God provides renders protection from temptation and the evil one. Faithfulness in wearing *all* the armor, not just part, makes the believer invulnerable. The armor is to be "put on" (the Greek is ingressive aorist imperative, meaning it is to be done urgently and immediately). It is only to the degree that we clothe ourselves with the full armor of God that we can contend successfully against the "wiles of the devil."

Dr. Martyn Lloyd Jones stated, "If you are to be a soldier in this army, if you are to fight victoriously in this crusade, you have to put on the entire equipment given to you. That is a rule in any army...And that is infinitely more true in this spiritual realm and warfare with which we are concerned...because your understanding is inadequate. It is God alone who knows your enemy, and He knows exactly the provision that is essential to you if you are to continue standing. Every single part and portion of this armor is absolutely essential; and the first thing you have to learn is that you are not in a position to pick and choose."[24]

The Belt of Truth

Soldiers wore a tunic of loose fitting cloth. In order that they would not be tripped up by it in battle, the loose ends would be pulled up and stashed in the girdle or belt. Spiritually the believer, based upon the truth of God's Word, is to pull in from his life hypocrisy and evil conduct, tucking them securely away lest they impede and hamper (Hebrews 12:1).

The Breastplate of Righteousness

I named my firstborn after the famous Scottish pastor Robert Murray McCheyne. McCheyne prayed a prayer that has long since become mine and I hope hitherto will become yours. He prayed, "O God, make me as holy as a pardoned sinner can be." To stand against the evil one and to finish life strong we must pursue holiness in attitude and action.

William Barclay declares, "When a man is clothed in righteousness he is impregnable. Words are no defense against accusations, but a good life is."[25]

Aging Honorably and Happily

The Gospel Shoes

The soldier needed shoes both to protect his feet from stones and briers and for stability in battle. We need a sure foundation lest our footing is lost and we suffer defeat. And what is that foundation?

S. J. Stone identifies it in the hymn "The Church's One Foundation."

> The church's one foundation is Jesus Christ, her Lord;
>> She is His new creation by water and the Word.
> From Heaven He came and sought her to be His holy bride;
>> With His own blood He bought her, and for her life He died.

Are you anchored to this foundation?

The Shield of Faith

Believers must continuously believe God [have faith] when assailed with lies spawned by the Devil.

Warren Wiersbe states, "True Bible faith is not blind optimism or a manufactured 'hope-so' feeling. True Bible faith is confident obedience to God's Word in spite of circumstances and consequences. This faith operates quite simply. God speaks, and we hear His Word. We trust His Word and act on it no matter what the circumstances are or what the consequences may be. The circumstances may be impossible and the consequences frightening and unknown, but we obey God's Word just the same and believe Him to do what is right and what is best."[26]

Absolute trust in God can retard the fiery darts of discouragement, depression, disillusionment, and temptation propelled from the pits of Hell.

Andrew Murray voices a prayer that all ought to pray with regard to their faith. "O Lord Jesus who art the Prince of the army of the Lord, the Hero, the Victor, teach me to be strong in Thee, my stronghold, and in the power of Thy might. Teach me to understand what the good fight of faith is and how the one thing that I have need of is always to look to Thee, to Thee, the supreme Guide of faith. And, consequently, in me too let this be the victory that overcometh the world, namely, my faith. Amen."[27]

Paul states the Christian's power word in confronting the enemy is the matchless name of Jesus. He says, "Therefore God also has highly exalted Him and given Him the name which is above every name, that at the name of Jesus every knee should bow, of those in heaven, and of those on earth, and of those under the earth, and *that* every tongue should confess that Jesus Christ *is* Lord, to the glory of God the Father." (Philippians 2:9–11 NKJV). The Devil and demons recognize the power and authority in the name of Jesus and must flee when it is spoken.

The Helmet of Salvation

To possess full confidence in the knowledge that you have been "born again," that you are a child of God saved for all time and eternity, grants power against the assaults of Satan.

The Sword of the Spirit

This Sword is the Word of God by which we thwart temptation's power, desist from sin, and aggressively attack the sins of the day. Barclay is right in saying, "We can never win God's battles without God's book."[28]

The Knees of Prayer

The preacher George Allen Smith was standing on the precipice of a mountain in the Alps viewing Switzerland when a gushing wind suddenly arose that threatened to blow him over the edge. Immediately his guide cried out, "Mr. Smith! On your knees, sir! The only way you're safe up here is on your knees!" When battling Satan, the only way you're safe down here is on your knees. Paul instructs, "Praying always with all prayer and supplication in the Spirit, and watching thereunto with all perseverance" (Ephesians 6:18).

E. M. Bounds wrote, "We can curtail our praying and not realize the peril until the foundations are gone. Hurried devotion makes weak faith, feeble convictions, and questionable piety. To be little with God is to do little for God."[29]

C. H. Spurgeon stated, "All Hell is vanquished when the believer bows his knee in importunate supplication. Beloved brethren, let us pray. We cannot all argue, but we can all pray; we cannot all be leaders, but we can all be pleaders; we cannot all be mighty in rhetoric, but we can all be prevalent in prayer."[30]

It is prayer that blows the sails of our vessel across the finish line triumphantly.

Spurgeon Finished Well

Upon news of C. H. Spurgeon's death in 1892, condolences flooded his home. This "Prince of Preachers" as he was widely known won thousands to Christ during his lifespan and left behind more sermons in print than any man present or past. He was known for his meekness, kindness, tenderness, and strong stand upon the Word of God. History acclaims Spurgeon as the greatest preacher in the past five hundred years. His life was plagued with severe illnesses and depression medically and with opposition theologically. Nonetheless he stayed the course to the end. "Two or three days before the end he said to his secretary, 'My work is done,' and after that he had nothing to do but to await the summons."[31]

A great tribute to Spurgeon's life was engraved upon his olive casket. The words were that of the Apostle Paul: "I have fought a good fight, I have finished my course, I have kept the faith."

Finish Strong—Finish Well

Charles Haddon Spurgeon ran an exemplary race in the faith and finished well. He sought not the accolades, applauds or awards of man but the Savior's embrace at the finish line with Him saying, "Well done, thou good and faithful servant."

And that's our purpose and goal in running the race.

Graham Is Finishing Well

Will Graham states of his grandfather, Billy Graham, "For me, when I sit and contemplate my grandfather, Billy Graham, I think that one of the greatest gifts he has given me in his twilight years is something more subtle (than his looks, legacy, worldview or possessions). He's given me a lesson. You see, this wonderful and godly man...is constantly teaching me an amazing lesson, and that lesson is how to finish well.

"One day my grandfather's 'time of departure' will come. He's fighting the good fight, he's finishing the race, and he's keeping the faith. He's ready for eternity. He's finishing well."[32]

All Have a Finish Line

John "the Penguin" Bingham is a marathon motivator; he motivates runners to successfully run marathons. He states, "As I stand at the starting line, I know that somewhere out there is a finish line." There is a finish line for each of us "somewhere out there." It may be ten or twenty years off, or ten or twenty days. The bottom line is that we acknowledge it and determine to cross it triumphantly.

How Will You Be Remembered?

Upon the 1993 suicidal death of Vincent Foster, adviser to Bill Clinton, the president said, "It would be wrong to define a life like Vincent Foster's in terms only of how it ended." Nevertheless, that's how Foster will be remembered—by how he finished the race. It may not be right, but people remember us for how we end the race more than how we ran it.

Aging Honorably and Happily

How do you want to be remembered? What do you hope people will say about you after you are gone? How will the people who knew you best summarize the 50 or 60 or 70 or 80 years of your life? Will they remember you as one who fainted in the last lap or completed the race well as Spurgeon did and Graham is doing?

Thomas S. Jones, Jr., poetically pictures a man who in the latter years of life ceases to be who he was earlier.

> Across the fields of yesterday
>   He sometimes comes to me,
> A little lad just back from play
>   The lad I used to be.
>
> And yet he smiles so wistfully
>   Once he has crept within.
> I wonder if he hopes to see
>   The man I might have been. ~ Thomas S. Jones, Jr.

God help us not to end life like that.

Examination Time

Oswald Chambers poses a most searching question for each to ask: "Am I getting nobler, better, more helpful, more humble as I get older? Am I exhibiting the life that men take knowledge of as having been with Jesus, or am I getting more self-assertive, more deliberately determined to have my own way? It is a great thing to tell yourself the truth."[33] And I add, if the first part of his question is not true of you, then while it is still possible, determine that it shall be.

Remember, as Yogi Berra put it, "It's not over till it's over." Fight the good fight of faith to the end. Finish well. Finish strong.

Just for laughs

A doctor speaking to a patient informed him that he had bad news and really bad news. The patient inquired about the bad news first. The doctor said the bad news is that you have twenty-four hours to live. The patient then inquired about the really bad news. The doctor replied, "I forgot to call you yesterday to tell you the bad news."

Getting married is like getting a telephone call in the middle of the night. First you get the ring; then you wake up.

From this battle there is no escape; from this hard service there is no discharge. It is a lifelong battle.[34] ~ Harry John Wilmot-Buxton

I would suppose God's greatest gift to a man, [is] that in his last days he have strength to serve the Lord God.[35] ~ W. A. Criswell

They will still yield fruit in old age. ~ Psalm 92:14 (NASB)

May no man ever look on me and say, "She lives, but all her usefulness is past."[36] ~ Ella Wheeler Wilcox

Retirement age is supposed to mean that I should sit in a rocking chair, wait for my social security check, and reminisce about the good old days. I have no thought of retiring. I would say with Caleb, "...give me this mountain..."! (Joshua 14:12). I am not asking for molehills. Old soldiers need not fade away. I have asked like Hezekiah for an extension of time; like Jabez, for an enlargement of coast; like Elisha, for an enduement of power. Caleb did not suffer, like the ten frightened spies, from a grasshopper complex. Too many cowards are cringing before the giants of Anak. God give us Caleb's looking for mountains to conquer![37] ~ Vance Havner.

3

Rethinking Retirement

Henry Wadsworth Longfellow was asked to write a poem in celebration of the fiftieth anniversary of the class of 1825 in Bowdoin College of which he was a graduate. He entitled it *"Morituri Salutamus"* (Latin for "We who are about to die salute thee.")

But why, you ask me, should this tale be told
To men grown old or who are growing old?
It is too late! Ah, nothing is too late
Till the tired heart shall cease to palpitate.

Cato learned Greek at eighty; Sophocles
Wrote his grand Oedipus, and Simonides
Bore off the prize of verse from his compeers,
When each had numbered more than fourscore years;
And Theophrastus, at fourscore and ten,
Had but begun his *Characters of Men.*

Chaucer, at Woodstock with the nightingales,
At sixty wrote the *Canterbury Tales;*
Goethe at Weimar, toiling to the last,
Completed *Faust* when eighty years were past.
For age is opportunity no less
Than youth itself, though in another dress,
And as the evening twilight fades away
The sky is filled with stars, invisible by day.

The coins in Spain long ago were stamped with the two pillars of Hercules which were the representative of the two promontories of the rock of Gibraltar. A scroll over the figure was stamped with the words, *"Ne plus ultra"* ("No more beyond"). Following the voyage of Columbus far beyond those pillars discovering the new world, Spain changed the coins' imprint. The word *"Ne"* was removed, leaving "plus ultra" ("more beyond").

Perhaps you think retirement means *"Ne plus ultra"*; there's nothing more you can do. But in reality it is *"plus ultra"* for much awaits you to do. An old writer states, "The work which a Christian man does in his closing years of life often has a spiritual vitality in it which that of his busier manhood had not. There is service still to render in the ministry of life that exemplifies the gifts of the Spirit—a service that is more abundant in its fruitage than those who bestow it realize."[38]

Counter the cultural view of retirement by forgoing the rocking chair, checkers game and pining away about yesterday. Though eighty-five years of age, Caleb wasn't about ready to throw in the towel on what he yet could do for the Lord. Neither must you. Express gratitude for past mountaintops of accomplishment, but with Caleb ever eye a new one. Certainly you have the ability, drive and passion to scale one more mountain, attain another victory, acquire another possession, accomplish one more feat and win one more battle for Christ whatever your age.

In God's Plan

Scaling mountains outside God's plan results in failure. Besides, at our age doing so is a waste of valuable time, energy and resources which are limited and rapidly passing.

In 1546, Michelangelo consented to the role of chief architect of the Basilica of St. Peter's in Rome, Italy, when more than seventy years old. In a letter to his grandnephew Buonarroti he wrote, "Many believe—and I believe—that I have been designated for this work by God. In spite of my old age, I do not want to give it up; I work out of love for God, and I put all my hope in Him."[39]

Rethinking Retirement

With Michelangelo, identify the mountain (ministry task) of God's designation and then exhibit faith in the mountain's acquisition. Don't stagger in unbelief. Don't look at the obstacles or difficulties. Rather, believe God will give it into your hands according to His will. Hebron (the mountain Caleb claimed) was yet in possession of giants, the Anakim. Nonetheless Caleb fearlessly in faith says, "Give me this mountain...." Caleb's faith gives way to work, and the mountain is acquired.

The pivotal key to Caleb's success was that he 'wholeheartedly followed the Lord.' To make the best of the twilight years of life you must do the same. John MacArthur states, "There's no value in being old if you're not godly. There's no value in being old if you're not a model or an example."[40] And I add, there is no value in being old if you've given up, hung up your cleats, turned in the keys and posted the sign "Do not Disturb."

Every season of life has its divine purpose, including that of the *golden years*. To simply *retire* to a rocking chair, bucket list, bingo at the recreational center, travel or be a recluse is a tragic waste of the treasure of a lifetime in knowledge, experience and service that yet can be of great benefit to the kingdom of God. Arouse yourself to take hold of that which God would have you accomplish in these latter years and finish life well.

The group of people in the church that has the greatest accumulation of experience in various ministry capacities (teaching, singing, soul winning, administration, leadership, finances) is the aged saints. The church sorely needs these godly saints not to resign their positions but re-sign to continue in them. These saints certainly are the spiritual and moral compass of the church and its ministry backbone.

Ralph Winter in his article "The Retirement Booby Trap" states, "Most men don't die of old age; they die of retirement. I read somewhere that half the men retiring in the state of New

Aging Honorably and Happily

York die within two years. Save your life and you'll lose it. Just like other drugs, other psychological addictions, retirement is a virulent disease, not a blessing....Where in the Bible do they see that? Did Moses retire? Did Paul retire? Peter? John? Do military officers retire in the middle of a war?"[41]

The Levites practiced a modified form of retirement (Numbers 8:23–26). It involved reduction in workload but not its abdication. We would do well to allow it to be our retirement model. As Dr. Frank Stagg aptly states about workload in retirement, "'All or nothing' is not an unbreakable law."[42] Certainly there is a happy and useful medium that lies between "All" and "Nothing" in service to the Lord.

Someone said, "God sends His servants to bed when they have done their work." Our journey is not done; our work is yet incomplete until God sends us to bed.

> Does the road wind uphill all the way?
>> Yes, to the very end.
> Will the day's journey take the whole long day?
>> From morn to night, my friend. ~ Christina Rossetti,
>>> 1830–1894

Duties of the Aged According to C. H. Spurgeon

Testimony is the duty of old men and women; they should labor whenever they can to bear testimony to God's faithfulness and to declare that now also, when they are old and grey-headed, their God forsakes them not.

There is another duty which is peculiarly the work of the aged, and that is the work of comforting the young believer. When the young Christian comes to them they say, "Do not fear. I have gone through the waters, and they have not overflown me; and through the fire, and have not been burned. Trust in God; for down to old age He is the same, and to hoar hairs He will carry you."

There is no one more qualified that I know of than kind-hearted old men to convert the young.

Then there is another work that is the work of the old, and that is the work of warning. If an old man were to go out in the middle of the road and shout out to you to stop, you would stop sooner than you would if a boy were to do it; for then you might say, "Out of the way, you young rascal," and go on still. The warnings of the old have great effect; and it is their peculiar work to guide the imprudent and warn the unwary.[43]

Biblical Examples of the Aged Serving God

"Scripture is filled," states Billy Graham, "with examples of men and women whom God used late in life, often with great impact—men and women who refused to use old age as an excuse to ignore what God wanted them to do."[44]

For example:

Moses and Aaron were chosen to lead the Israelites out of Egyptian bondage at the ages of 80 and 83 (Exodus 7:7).

Joshua was chosen to direct the conquest of Canaan during the last thirty years of his life. He died at age 110 (Joshua 24:29).

Caleb was involved in the conquest of Canaan with Joshua while in his eighties (Joshua 14:10).

Daniel served the Lord for over 70 years (Daniel 1:21) and was well over 80 when serving as one of the three governors over the kingdom of Babylon (Daniel 6:1–3).

Zacharias and Elizabeth, the parents of John the Baptist, were "both well advanced in years" (Luke 1:7) while Zacharias was serving still in the Temple.

Aging Honorably and Happily

Paul in Philemon 9 refers to himself as "the aged" (KJV), "old man" (NLT), "an elderly man" (Holman); yet he had not slowed down in ministry, for while in prison he was writing letters (Ephesians, Colossians, Philippians, Philemon), and upon release resumed ministry among the saints.

> It is not for us who are passengers to meddle with the chart and with the compass. Let that all-skilled Pilot alone with His own work. ~ Hall

Jonah's Mountain

The *Global Prayer Digest* shares the story of Jonah, a 73-year-old Chinese evangelist, who has traveled around the People's Republic spreading the Good News about Jesus Christ. "His days are full and his energy unflagging. In one weekend Jonah may bicycle nine hours, spend 40 hours on a hard railway seat and eight hours on a bumpy bus just to bring the message of Jesus Christ to people in remote villages or to urban churches with 5,000 members or to young soldiers....The schedule is grueling, but 73-year-old Jonah says, 'Rest is for the next world.'"[45]

J. Oswald Sanders

J. Oswald Sanders (1902–1992) was General Director of Overseas Missionary Fellowship. At age eighty-nine he said that he had written a book a year since he was seventy. Fortunately he didn't buy into the cultural retirement philosophy, else the church would have been the poorer. Upon hearing of his discipline in old age to so write, I determined by God's help I would attempt the same. I don't want to waste my final years. How about you?

John Wesley

John Wesley (1703–1791) in forty years of ministry traveled over 250,000 miles on horseback, preaching over 40,000 sermons.

Rethinking Retirement

At age eighty-three he was annoyed that he was unable to write more than fifteen hours a day without hurting his eyes, and at age eighty-six ashamed if he failed to preach more than twice a day.

Thomas Scott

Thomas Scott (1747–1821) was an influential preacher and author who is principally known for his best-selling work *A Commentary on the Whole Bible*. He began the study of Hebrew at the age of eighty-seven.

Michelangelo

Michelangelo (1475-1564) was a sculptor, painter and architect considered to be one of the greatest artists of the Italian Renaissance period. At age ninety Michelangelo painted the ceiling of Sistine Chapel on his back on a scaffold. How impressive is that!

God needs more seniors to be like these men, those who press their body, mind and strength to the limit in ministry endeavors that more may know Christ.

Remembering that God is owner of every stage of life, resolve to submit joyfully and willingly to that which He wants you to do in this stage as in all the prior ones. There is no discharge or retirement in serving the Lord, only promotion to Heaven or desertion.

Lord, when thou seest that my work is done,
Let me not linger on with failing powers
Adown the weary hours,
A workless worker in a world of work.
But with a word just bid me home
And I will come.
Right gladly—yea, right gladly—
Will I come. ~ John Oxenham

Aging Honorably and Happily

Now, press your feet into the sod, throw your shoulder's erect, set your face as a flint, and say with Caleb, "O God, 'Give me [one more] mountain' before I make my exodus."

We'll work till Jesus comes;
We'll work till Jesus comes;
We'll work till Jesus comes,
And we'll be gathered home. ~ Elizabeth K. Mills

Just for Laughs

A grandson asked his grandfather how old he was. He teasingly replied, "I'm not sure."

"Look in your underwear, Grandpa," he advised. "Mine says I'm 4 to 6."

A king irritated by his court jester sentenced him to death without giving it serious thought. Upon realizing the rashness of his decree, the king said to the court jester, "In consideration of your faithful services, I will permit you to select the manner in which you prefer to die."

The Court Jester instantly answered: "I elect to die of old age."[46]

Keep yourselves in the love of God. ~ Jude 1:21

You can't help getting older, but you don't have to get old.
~ George Burns

Nobody grows old merely by living a number of years. We grow old by deserting our ideals. Years may wrinkle the skin, but to give up enthusiasm wrinkles the soul.[47] ~ Samuel Ullman

It is possible to be happy without having perfect health.... Thank goodness my happiness doesn't come from my joints, but from my heart.[48] ~ Beverley LaHaye

In biblical perspective and incontestably, the best time to get ready to be old is as soon as possible.[49] ~ Frank Stagg

4

Resolutions on Growing Old

Here are my *Ten Resolutions on Growing Old with God* based upon Psalm 71 that I heartily commend to you.

1) I will ditch the talk about my aches and pains and speak of God's greatness and goodness. God and man alike hate a grumbler, whiner and complainer. "My lips shall greatly rejoice when I sing unto thee; and my soul, which thou hast redeemed" (v. 23).

Avoid a Grumbling Tongue. "And when the people complained, it displeased the LORD: and the LORD heard it" (Numbers 11:1). To God's displeasure, the Israelites complained and grumbled in the wilderness about His manner of provision for their needs. I certainly don't want that to be my disposition in old age.

There are few things worse than hearing Christians grumble and complain in light of all God has done and is doing for them. The chorus to "The Grumbler's Song" describes them:

Oh, they grumble on Monday, Tuesday, Wednesday,
Grumble on Thursday too.
They grumble on Friday, Saturday, Sunday,
Grumble the whole week through.

I intend to heed Spurgeon's counsel in his saying, "Do not let the young people catch you indulging in melancholy, sitting in your chimney corner, grumbling and growling; but go about cheerful and happy, and they will think how blessed it is to be a Christian. If you are surly and fretful, they will think the Lord has forsaken you; but keep a smiling countenance, and they will think the promise is fulfilled: 'And even to your old age I am he; and even to hoar hairs will I carry you: I have made, and I will bear; even I will carry, and will deliver you' (Isaiah 46:4)."[50]

Aging Honorably and Happily

In light of God's gracious provision, Jeremiah asks a most pressing question: "Then why should we, mere humans, complain?" (Lamentations 3:39 NLT). God keep me from becoming a complainer regarding Him, family, others, and/or my circumstances in old age.

2) I will reminisce about God's goodness to me continuously. "My tongue also shall talk of thy righteousness all the day long" (v. 24). With Charles Wesley I will say,

> Oh, for a thousand tongues to sing
>   My great Redeemer's praise,
> The glories of my God and King,
>   The triumphs of his grace!

"Christians have many treasures," says C. H. Spurgeon, "to lock up in the cabinet of memory."[51] And in old age I intend to open the cabinet recalling God's manifold goodness unto me throughout life. As I do, my heart certainly will swell with praise shouting with the psalmist, "I bless the holy name of God with all my heart. Yes, I will bless the Lord and not forget the glorious things he does for me. He forgives all my sins. He heals me. He ransoms me from hell. He surrounds me with loving-kindness and tender mercies. He fills my life with good things! My youth is renewed like the eagle's" (Psalm 103:1–5 TLB)!

3) I will exhibit hope and trust in God as I did in my youth, stubbornly refusing to yield to despair or depression despite frailty or infirmity or abode in a nursing home or hospital. "For thou art my hope, O Lord GOD: thou art my trust from my youth" (v. 5).

> My life is but a weaving
>   Between my God and me.
> I cannot choose the colors
>   He weaveth steadily.

Resolutions on Growing Old

Oft' times He weaveth sorrow,
    And I in foolish pride
Forget He sees the upper
    And I the underside.

Not 'til the loom is silent
    And the shuttles cease to fly
Will God unroll the canvas
    And reveal the reason why.

The dark threads are as needful
    In the weaver's skillful hand
As the threads of gold and silver
    In the pattern He has planned

He knows, He loves, He cares;
    Nothing this truth can dim.
He gives the very best to those
    Who leave the choice to Him. ~ Corrie ten Boom

4) I will look to God, not man or unto my own self, as a refuge in the time of difficulty, suffering, sorrow and sickness. "Be thou my strong habitation, whereunto I may continually resort…for thou art my rock and my fortress…[and] my strong refuge" (v. 3, 7).

Solomon states that God's name is "like a strong tower" that keeps us safe and secure from the enemy (Proverbs 18:10). A tower in biblical days provided protection for people in times of different types of emergencies. God's name is like that strong tower for the saved. In times of emergencies (all sorts of trouble or crisis or problems), when the believer calls on God's name, He will grant protection. This tower is so deep that no bomb can undermine it, so thick that no missile can penetrate it, so high that no ladder can scale it or arrow of Hell reach it (Psalm 27:5).

Aging Honorably and Happily

I am resolved to run into this strong tower in the time of difficulty to find comfort, peace, help and hope.

Stand up, stand up for Jesus; stand in His strength alone.
The arm of flesh will fail you; ye dare not trust your own.
~ George Duffield, Jr.

5) I will pray more. "Incline thine ear unto me, and save me" (v.2). Prayer is the never failing means whereby the believer is sustained physically, strengthened spiritually and renewed mentally. Thomas Watson said, "Prayer delights God's ear; it melts His heart and opens His hand. God cannot deny a praying soul."[52]

In old age there is more time to pray and more for which to pray. With Andrew Murray I want "the place of secret prayer [to] become to me the most beloved spot on earth."[53]

6) I will not compromise the biblical convictions of my youth but will fully adhere to them. "O God, thou hast taught me from my youth" (v. 17). Old age is not the time to backpedal on biblical principles and beliefs taught and embraced in younger years. Additionally, I resolve to spend more time in the Word soaking in its spiritual nutrients which enhance life to its fullest.

7) Instead of wavering, I resolve to press on passionately and with perseverance in order to finish well. "O God, be not far from me: O my God, make haste for my help" (v. 12). Polycarp said, "Eighty and six years have I served Him, and He never wronged me; and shall I forsake my God and my Savior?" I determine to end life with likeminded fortitude.

8) I will tell of the Lord more than ever. "My mouth shall shew forth thy righteousness and thy salvation all the day" (v.15). Instead of my keeping silent in old age about Jesus, may He enable me many opportunities to win souls whether the pulpit be a church or hospital, wheelchair or nursing home. I claim the

Resolutions on Growing Old

promise of Psalm 92:14 which states, "Even in old age they will still produce fruit; they will remain vital and green" (NLT).

In old age and poor health Dr. John R. Rice wrote a Christmas letter to friends in which he expressed his burning passion. He wrote: "I still, from my armchair, preach in great revival campaigns. I still envision hundreds walking the aisles to accept Christ. *I still feel hot tears for the lost.* I still see God working miracles. I want no Christmas without a burden for lost souls, a message for sinners, a heart to bring in the lost sheep so dear to the Shepherd, the sinning souls for whom Christ died. May food be tasteless and music a discord and Christmas a farce if I forget the dying millions to whom I am debtor, if this fire in my bones does not still flame! Not till I die or not till Jesus comes will I ever be eased of this burden, these tears, this toil to save souls."[54]

In old age, as with Rice, I want to maintain the soul winner's passion and heart endeavoring to reach the lost regardless of cost or consequence or human frailty.

9) I will look for the silver lining of blessing in the woes of life I must experience and render praise unto the Lord. "Thou, which hast shewed me great and sore troubles, shalt quicken me again" (v. 20). I want to display faith in the fire, trusting God to be with me in its midst, bringing glory to His name and using it for good in my life (Romans 8:28).

Max Lucado offers a word of godly counsel regarding suffering that I want to always embrace. He states, "A season of suffering is a small assignment when compared to the reward. Rather than begrudge your problem, explore it. Ponder it. And most of all, use it. Use it to the glory of God."[55] It is not always easy to accept all things that happen and/or receive them with thanksgiving (Ephesians 5:20), but by God's grace that is my intent.

Aging Honorably and Happily

Kirk Cameron offers hope and comfort in the hour of trial. He shares, "God steps into the suffering with us, and He takes it on himself, and He walks through it with us, and He uses it to create something in you that is unstoppable."[56]

10) I will resist evolving into the *stereotypes* of old people and becoming like many who are elderly (grouchy, critical, complaining, negative, cantankerous, unproductive, self-centered, or overly demanding). Dr. Frank Staggs says, "Nothing so damages human existence and makes the later years emptier or more miserable than garden-variety selfishness. On the other hand, just look around at older people whose lives are radiant in power and beauty. They are not selfish people. They are people who have found life by giving it to God and to the service of other people."[57] May God protect me from being a selfish old man.

"Thou shalt increase my greatness, and comfort me on every side. I will also praise thee with the psaltery, even thy truth, O my God: unto thee will I sing with the harp, O thou Holy One of Israel. My lips shall greatly rejoice when I sing unto thee; and my soul, which thou hast redeemed" (vv. 21–23).

In old age I want my countenance and conduct to reflect His presence in me. I am not a singer, but I want to join the psalmist in being a singer in old age praising God for manifold blessings, comfort and salvation.

Psalm 5:11 (ESV): "Let all who take refuge in you rejoice; let them ever sing for joy, and spread your protection over them, that those who love your name may exult in you."

Psalm 9:2: "I will be glad and rejoice in thee: I will sing praise to thy name, O thou most High."

Psalm 51:14 (ESV): "Deliver me from bloodguiltiness, O God, O God of my salvation, and my tongue will sing aloud of your righteousness."

Resolutions on Growing Old

Psalm 59:16: "I will sing of thy power; yea, I will sing aloud of thy mercy in the morning: for thou hast been my defence and refuge in the day of my trouble."

Psalm 63:7 (ESV): "For you have been my help, and in the shadow of your wings I will sing for joy."

Sometimes joy births singing; sometimes singing births joy. Therefore, in whatever state I find myself I want to engage in singing unto the Lord. It is medicine to the soul.

A song drilled into me in youth choir years ago yet is remembered:

Sing, make a joyful sound;
Sing, new life in Christ is found.
Now in my heart He reigns. Sing! Sing! Sing!

Perhaps the final hymn Philip Bliss wrote before his tragic death in a train wreck is *My Redeemer* in which he exhorts the saved to sing.

Sing, oh, sing of my Redeemer;
    With His blood He purchased me.
On the cross, He sealed my pardon,
    Paid the debt, and made me free. ~ Philip Bliss

Additionally I never want to become like "the old and foolish king" Solomon referenced who refused to learn anything new (Ecclesiastes 4:13). In old age I want to keep studying the Word personally and listening to biblical teachers and preachers, that I might ever increase my knowledge of God and His Word.

How well I will do with these resolutions only time will tell. But I certainly am intending with determination to keep them. How about you?

Aging Honorably and Happily

Just for laughs

A pastor was visiting an elderly person in the nursing home when he saw a bowl of nuts near her bedside. He began eating the nuts until they were all gone. Realizing what he had done he told the lady he was sorry for eating all her nuts. The lady replied, "That's okay. I already finished sucking all the chocolate off of them."

A wife complains to her husband: "Just look at that couple down the road, how loving they are. He keeps holding her hand, kissing her, holding the door for her. Why can't you do the same?" The husband: "Are you mad? I barely know that woman!"[58]

Has this world been so kind to you that you should leave with regret? There are better things ahead than any we leave behind.[59] ~ C. S. Lewis

If you are a Christian, you are not a citizen of this world trying to get to Heaven; you are a citizen of Heaven making your way through this world.[60] ~ Vance Havner

An aged Christian, with the snow of time upon his head, may remind us that those points of earth are whitest which are nearest to heaven.[61] ~ Edwin Hubbel Chapin

I am hard pressed · between the two, in that I have the desire to depart and be with Christ, for that is much better by far. ~ Apostle Paul (Philippians 1:23 Mounce)

5

The Alternative to Getting Old

Who wants to grow old? Comedian George Burns, who lived to be over one hundred, quipped, "It's better than the alternative." But Burns was wrong, for the alternative for the believer is far better. It means arrival at our new Home to be forever with the Lord and the redeemed.

Heaven

Jesus said Heaven is a place.

It is a physical place (John 14:2). It is a place just as much as the city in which you reside is a place. If it were not, the Bible would not speak of its streets of pure gold, walls of jasper, foundations of twelve precious stones and gates of pearl, or its inhabitants. To the liberals who claim this description of Heaven is simply figurative language, Jesus responds, "If it were not so, I would have told you." In other words, Jesus is saying, "If Heaven were not like I described it, I would have told you so!"

It is a promised place (John 14:3), and God never fails to keep His promise. The apostle Paul affirms this truth: "In hope of eternal life, which God, that cannot lie, promised before the world began" (Titus 1:2).

It is a perfect place (Revelation 22:3–5) free from the curse of sin and the ravaging of Satan and his cohorts.

It is a pleasurable place (Revelation 5:9). "Heaven will not be the boring experience of strumming a harp on a cloud, as some facetiously characterize it," stated Paul Little. He continues, "It will be the most dynamic, expanding, exhilarating experience conceivable. Our problem now is that, with our finite minds, we cannot imagine it."[62]

Aging Honorably and Happily

The theologian Jon Courson makes an excellent observation. "When Jesus says, 'I go to prepare a place for you,' He is not speaking generically, but specifically. Jesus is preparing a place for you specifically. Think through this. What do you enjoy? What has God built into your being? Whatever it is, know this. Jesus is preparing a place for you to fulfill the elements He's woven into the fabric of your personality uniquely and specifically."[63]

It is a permanent place (2 Corinthians 5:8). The apostle Paul states, "Then we which are alive and remain shall be caught up together with them in the clouds, to meet the Lord in the air: and so shall we *ever* be with the Lord" (1 Thessalonians 4:17).

With all that is known to man about Heaven, there is so much that is unknown that only adds to its grandeur.

What great saints state about Heaven

R. G. Lee said, "The word *meager* means 'deficient in or destitute of quantity and quality.' When I use the word *meagerness* in pointing to Heaven, I mean to say that any quantity of words, most skillfully arranged and most eloquently spoken, are deficient in power fully to portray the wonders and wealth of the place called Heaven."[64] Lee continues, "If there were an island somewhere on earth where all forms of cancer were mysteriously cured, AIDS could be completely healed, hearts never failed, arthritis never inflamed a joint, cholesterol never clogged an artery, and death never visited a family, you would give everything you owned to be on that island. And yet multitudes look scoffingly at Heaven, which is just such a place."[65]

T. DeWitt Talmage said, "My Heaven is a solid Heaven. After the resurrection has come, you will have a resurrected foot and something to tread on, and a resurrection eye and colors to see with it, and a resurrection ear and music to regale it....I have no patience with your transcendental, gelatinous, gaseous heaven."

The Alternative to Getting Old

C. H. Spurgeon states, "The old clay shed will be taken down, and you shall dwell in marble halls! You shall leave the hovel for the mansion! The traveler's tent shall be rolled up and put away in the tomb to be exchanged for 'a house not made with hands, eternal in the heavens.' May Divine Grace cause you so to set this house in order that you may leave it without reluctance and enter into the next with joy, leaving your first house behind you without shame in sure and certain hope of a blessed resurrection! May you cheerfully leave the first house and joyfully surrender the key to the Great Landlord. Then, conveyed by ministering spirits to a better country, you shall become possessors of a heritage undefiled which fades not away!"[66]

He continues, "How different will be the state of the believer in Heaven from what it is here!...Ah, toil-worn laborer, only think when thou shalt rest forever! Canst thou conceive it? It is a rest eternal, a rest that 'remaineth.' Here my best joys bear 'mortal' on their brow, my fair flowers fade, my dainty cups are drained to dregs, my sweetest birds fall before Death's arrows, my most pleasant days are shadowed into nights, and the flood-tides of my bliss subside into ebbs of sorrow; but there, everything is immortal, the harp abides unrusted, the crown unwithered, the eye undimmed, the voice unfaltering, the heart unwavering, and the immortal being is wholly absorbed in infinite delight."[67]

Max Lucado said, "We may speak about a place where there are no tears, no death, no fear, no night; but those are just the benefits of Heaven. The beauty of Heaven is seeing God."[68]

Billy Graham states, "Our imaginations simply cannot comprehend the grandeur of this wonderful home, a place of everlasting joy, contentment, and peace."[69]

Don't lose sight of Heaven

Sometimes I think seniors get so wrapped up with their ills, losses, struggles, pains and fears that they lose sight of the fact that Heaven and all its preciousness awaits them. If saints but pondered more about where they are going instead of where they have been or presently are, then most if not all of the gloom-and-doom despair, self-pity and self-centered disposition they experience would vanish.

Richard Baxter echo's my conviction. "If there be so certain and glorious a rest for the saints, why is there no more industrious seeking after it? One would think if a man did but once hear of such unspeakable glory to be obtained and believed what he heard to be true, he should be transported with the vehemency of his desire after it and should almost forget to eat and drink and should care for nothing else and speak of and inquire after nothing else but how to get this treasure. And yet people who hear of it daily and profess to believe it as a fundamental article of their faith do as little mind it or labor for it as if they had never heard of any such thing or did not believe one word they hear."[70]

"As we grow older," Billy Graham states, "we should focus not only on the present, but more and more on Heaven. This world, with all of its pains and sorrows and burdens, isn't our final home. If we know Christ, we know we have 'an inheritance that can never perish, spoil or fade—kept in Heaven for you' (1 Peter 1:4). I know it won't be long before I'll be going there, and I look forward to that day. Heaven gives us hope and makes our present burdens easier to bear."[71]

Graham's words sound a whole like those of Paul's when he said, "So we are always confident, even though we know that as long as we live in these bodies we are not at home with the Lord. For we live by believing and not by seeing. Yes, we are fully confident, and we would rather be away from these earthly bodies, for then we will be at home with the Lord" (2 Corinthians 5:6-8, NLT).

Knowledge of a personal reservation in Heaven made by Jesus Christ ought to put believers on shouting ground and liber-

The Alternative to Getting Old

ate them from the shackles and chains of this world that unduly cause anxiety, worry, despair and discomfort.

> Sing the wondrous love of Jesus;
> Sing His mercy and His grace.
> In the mansions bright and blessed
> He'll prepare for us a place.
> When we all get to Heaven,
> What a day of rejoicing that will be!
> When we all see Jesus,
> We'll sing and shout the victory![72]

Meet me at the fountain

At the industrial exposition in Chicago many years ago was a fountain which served as a meeting place for friends. One would say to a friend, "Will you meet me at the fountain?" The reply was, "All right, I will meet you at the fountain." The hymn writer P. P. Bliss wrote a gospel song based on the fountain, elevating the thought from the physical (exposition ground) to the spiritual (Heaven).

> Will you meet me at the fountain
> When I reach the glory-land?
> When you meet me at the fountain
> Shall I clasp your friendly hand?
>
> Other friends will give you welcome;
> Other loving voices cheer.
> There'll be music at the fountain—
> Will you, will you meet me there?

I am looking forward to rendezvousing with you at the fountain. Make sure you have the reservation!

Aging Honorably and Happily

Just for laughs

With the season of "old age" comes deterioration of many members of the body that hamper life as it once was. I read a story about three elderly people who were sitting in rocking chairs on the front porch of their rest home. One said to the others, "You know, I don't hear so well anymore, and I thought it would bother me more than it does. But there isn't much that I want to hear anyway."

The second woman said, "Yes, I've found the same with my eyes. Everything looks blurred and cloudy now, but I don't care. I saw just about everything that I wanted to see when I was younger."

The third lady thought for a moment and then said, "Well, I don't know about that. I sort of miss my mind."

Hearing voices in your head is normal. Listening to them is quite common. Arguing with them is acceptable. It is only when you lose that argument that you get into real trouble.[73]

If wrinkles must be written upon our brows, let them not be written upon the heart. The spirit should not grow old.[74] ~ President James A. Garfield

I shall grow old but never lose life's zest,
Because the road's last turn will be the best. ~ Henry Van Dyke

To the veteran soldier of the cross, old age must assuredly be a time of great joy and blessedness.[75] ~ C. H. Spurgeon

6

Remember My Chains

It is with exact purpose that upon finishing the dictation of the letter to the church at Colossae to his secretary (perhaps so dictated due to an eye-disorder or the difficulty of writing while chained to a Roman soldier) that Paul writes the final greeting "with my own hand." In the greeting he says, "Remember my chains" (Colossians 4:18).

Paul wanted the saints to understand and remember that his chains limited him as to what he could do for the Lord. Certainly older people can identify with Paul in his bondage, for they have a *chain* of some kind that hinders them also from doing more for Christ.

For some it's the chain of *sickness and disease*. The medically chained earnestly desire to do more for Christ, but their infirmities hinder them.

For some it's the chain of a *physical handicap*. The wheelchair, crutches, braces or an artificial limb serves as a chain restricting some service to Christ.

For some it's the chain of *money*. Most seniors are on a very limited income necessitating that they stretch every dollar to its furthest in order to meet their monthly needs. These deeply long to give more to God's work and servants but are bound financially from so doing.

For some it's the chain of *physical frailty*. As the body ages it becomes fragile, hindering one from doing things he once easily could. As seniors of all ages, we certainly identify with that!

For some it's the chain of *being a caregiver*. The task of caring for a sick spouse, child or parent 24/7 hampers and impedes much of what one desires to do for Christ.

Aging Honorably and Happily

For some it's the chain of a *job*. Sadly, due to economic and/or other issues, some seniors are forced back into the workforce to survive, and it chains them from doing more for the kingdom of God.

Observations

God understands our chains whether or not others do.

Most of our chains are invisible to others as theirs are to us.

Our brother's chain ought to be remembered. We all ought to endeavor to withhold judgment upon others based upon what is seen or thought but not fully known. Before you criticize or accuse another, walk a mile in his shoes (experience his chains). Do what you can to help others bear their chains.

Don't allow your chain to be a reason for self-pity, spiritual inactivity or gaining sympathy. Paul didn't, and his chain was far greater than your shackles.

Redeem the time. Paul's chains hindered him from doing what he *would* for Christ but not what he *could*. He desired to continue his missionary journey, but his chains prevented that happening, so he made the best of the opportunity at hand by preaching the Gospel to the soldiers to whom he was shackled. Despite not being able to do what you want to do (sing, preach, attend church, missionary service, etc.) due to chains, do what you can with them.

Stretch your chain to its furthest extent. It is no sin to be in bondage to a divinely allowed chain as long as you are using it to its fullest potential (something most fail to do).

Learn to be content and joyful in your chains. The chains bound Paul's hands not his heart. He said "Always be full of joy in the Lord. I say it again—rejoice!...Not that I was ever in need, for I have learned how to be content with whatever I have. I know how to live on almost nothing or with everything. I have learned the secret of living in every situation, whether it is with a full stomach or empty, with plenty or little. For I can do everything through Christ, who gives me strength" (Philippians 4:4; 11–13 NLT).

It's okay to pray for the removal of some chains. No doubt Paul in asking the saints to remember his chains was invoking them to pray for his release. Pray, expect and hope to be released from chains that hold you back from doing more for Christ. If it's God's will for the chains to remain, accept them as such and make the best of them.

Tension will only be evidenced when your chain is stretched as far as it possibly can reach. It is at this point you will know it is being used as best it can.

Fanny Crosby, blinded at six weeks old due to an incompetent doctor, had her *chain.* Yet she determined early in life it would not impact her joy or service to God. By the age of fifteen, Fanny could quote the first five books of the Bible, Proverbs, Song of Solomon and the four Gospels. At the time of her death she had composed over eight thousand hymns. She is an exemplary example of someone stretching her chain to its furthest extent though challenging and difficult.

Utilize your chain(s) to their furthest extent as Fanny Crosby did, and at the Judgment Seat you can say, "Lord, I didn't do all I wanted to do for you, but remember my bonds!" He then in reply will say, "Well done, thou good and faithful servant: thou hast been faithful over a few things, I will make thee ruler over many things: enter thou into the joy of thy Lord" (Matthew 25:21).

Just for laughs

An elderly couple was driving out to meet friends for a social evening when the wife said, "Honey, you try to remember where we're going, and I'll try to remember who we are."

Aging Honorably and Happily

A couple in their nineties had trouble remembering things. When they saw their doctor, he told them that they were both physically fine and advised them to write things down to help their memory. Later that day at home the husband asked his wife if she wanted a snack.

"Could you bring me a bowl of ice cream?" she asked.

"Sure," he replied.

"Do you think you should write that down to remember it?" she asked.

"No, I can remember that," he said.

"I'd like some strawberries on it, too. Do you need to write that down?" she asked.

"No, I can remember that, too. Ice cream with strawberries," he said, becoming a little irritated.

"I'd like some whipped cream on it, too. Can you remember all that? The doctor said you should write things down," she said.

"For goodness sake, I can remember that. I don't need to write it down. A bowl of ice cream with strawberries and whipped cream," he said, now more than a little irritated. Off he went to the kitchen. About twenty minutes later he returned with a plate of bacon and eggs.

The wife stared at it for a moment and said, "Where's my toast?"

As iron sharpens iron, so one person sharpens another. ~ Solomon

Wise counsel to the younger is the duty of the aged. ~ Unknown

Spiritually mature people in the Bible appear as mentors. Mentoring sketches in the Bible challenge members of the older generation to be capable mentors and the younger generation to accept the insights of aging mentors.[76] ~ J. Gordon Harris

There is nothing I like better than conversing with aged men, for I regard them as travelers who have gone a journey which I too may have to go, and of whom I ought to inquire whether the way is smooth and easy or rugged and difficult. Is life harder toward the end, or what report do you give it?[77] ~ Plato

I think older women not only have a tremendous privilege but a very great responsibility to talk to younger women, to try to help them realize what a blessing it is that they are that age, and then to testify to them what a blessing it is to be this age.[78] ~ Elizabeth Elliot

The gray head is a crown of glory if it be found in the way of righteousness. Somebody old who has walked a long time in the path of righteousness is a treasure, a treasure of wisdom and a treasure of experience and a treasure of understanding. A triumphant Christian who has fought the battle over and over and over and been victorious, who has experienced everything that the young are waiting to experience, becomes a great treasure to the church.[79] ~ John MacArthur

7

Mentoring the Younger

In the heart and mind of godly seniors there is a reservoir of the knowledge of God, the Bible, church, and finances; ministry and administration know-how; marital and parenting success secrets; and wisdom as to how to deal with trials and difficulties—things that the younger generation desperately needs. Transferal to another of what you have gained from experience and study in life is called mentoring.

Mentoring is the rewarding process of taking younger men/women under one's protective and provisional wings to edify, educate, embolden, emancipate, enlighten, establish, excite, and equip in spiritual matters. A mentor is a guide, instructor, and model to his mentee.

Mentoring is first mentioned in Scripture in God's command to Israel.

"Hear, O Israel: The LORD our God, the Lord is one. Love the Lord your God with all your heart and with all your soul and with all your strength. These commandments that I give you today are to be on your hearts. Impress them on your children. Talk about them when you sit at home and when you walk along the road, when you lie down and when you get up. Tie them as symbols on your hands and bind them on your foreheads. Write them on the doorframes of your houses and on your gates" (Deuteronomy 6:4–9 NIV).

In the New Testament the writer of Hebrews underscores the practice in stating, "And let us consider how we may spur one another on toward love and good deeds, not giving up meeting together, as some are in the habit of doing, but encouraging one another—and all the more as you see the Day approaching" (Hebrews 10:24–25 NIV).

Aging Honorably and Happily

A. W. Pink states of this text: "Here is expressed the chief design or end of our consideration for one another: it is to provoke or stir up unto the performance of duties; to strengthen zeal, to inflame affections, to excite unto godly living. We are to provoke one another by means of a godly example, by suitable exhortations, by unselfish acts of kindness. We are to fire one another "unto love," which is not a mere sentiment or natural affability, but a holy principle of action which seeks the highest good of its object."[80]

Paul instructs older women in the church to mentor the young women in regard to several matters (Titus 2:3–5). Older men likewise have an equal responsibility to mentor the younger men.

Examples of Mentoring

Barnabas mentored Paul. Luke writes, "But Barnabas took him [Paul], and brought him to the apostles, and declared unto them how he had seen the Lord in the way, and that he had spoken to him, and how he had preached boldly at Damascus in the name of Jesus" (Acts 9:27). The words "took him" literally mean that Barnabas physically held on to Paul to help him mature in the faith, and because he did so Paul became a great apostle and missionary.

Chuck Swindoll testifies, "I cannot overestimate the impact that a mentor can have in another life, and I am reminded of that anytime I look at my own. I am a living legacy to a handful of men who took an interest in me, saw potential where I did not, and encouraged me to become something more."

Charles Spurgeon, the greatest preacher of the nineteenth century, said of Mary King, the housekeeper at the school he attended as a teenager in Newmarket: "Many a time we have gone over the covenant of grace together and talked of the personal election of the saints, their union to Christ, their final perseverance, and what vital godliness meant; and I do believe that I learned more from her than I should have learned from any six doctors of divinity of the sort we have nowadays."

Charles Stanley states, "The power to impact others is not so much in what we do but in who we are. Throughout my life many people have helped shape my character, thoughts and behavior, though I don't always remember their specific words or actions. In turn, I want to make a positive impact on others, whether through a one-time encounter or a long-term relationship."[81]

Talk about the value of mentoring, here it is mightily displayed in the lives of Paul, Swindoll, Spurgeon and Stanley.

Competency to Mentor

Referring to mentoring, Paul said, "I myself am convinced, my brothers and sisters, that you yourselves are full of goodness, filled with knowledge and competent to instruct one another" (Romans 15:14 NIV). As with the Roman saints, you are competent to instruct others about the faith because of your life of spiritual and moral goodness, heart for God and reservoir of biblical knowledge.

Francis Chan said, "The church is in dire need of elderly people who are living radically for their faith. And some [of these] young people are dying to come under the tutelage of elderly people that seriously cannot wait to see Jesus and are living that way."[82]

Theological or counseling degrees or mentoring training are not required to be a mentor. Young husbands and fathers, wives and mothers, and singles in pursuit of God's design for their lives simply need someone who will lovingly walk with them answering their questions, guiding their decisions, modeling the faith, and providing encouragement and sometimes giving biblical instruction. The aged Christian certainly has what it takes to do this task.Solomon said, "Iron sharpeneth iron" (Proverbs 27:17). The Lord is counting on His people to sharpen the iron of young and middle-aged adults doctrinally, devotionally and dutifully until they then can do the same for another. Will you take seriously the Lord's command not only to win souls but to "make disciples" regardless of cost? At this season of your life, make room on your plate to invest in another's life, allowing the mighty rivers of your spiritual knowledge and experience to flow into them and then through them to the glory of God.

Just for Laughs

Seeing her friend Sally wearing a new locket, Meg asks if there was a memento of some sort inside.

"Yes," said Sally, "a lock of my husband's hair."

"But Larry's still alive."

"I know, but his hair is gone."[83]

The local news station was interviewing an eighty-year-old lady who had just gotten married for the fourth time. The interviewer asked her questions about her life, about what it felt like to be marrying again at eighty, and then about her new husband's occupation. "He's a funeral director," she answered. "Interesting," the newsman thought. He then asked her if she would mind telling him a little about her first three husbands and what they did for a living.

She paused for a few moments, needing time to reflect on all those years. After a short time a smile came to her face, and she answered proudly, explaining that she had first married a banker when she was in her 20s, then a circus ringmaster when in her

Mentoring the Younger

40s, and a preacher when in her 60s—and now in her 80s a funeral director.

The interviewer looked at her, quite astonished, and asked why she had married four men with such diverse careers. She smiled and explained, "I married one for the money, two for the show, three to get ready, and four to go."[84]

The memory of the righteous will be a blessing. ~ Proverbs 10:7

At age 20, we worry about what others think of us. At age 40, we don't care what they think of us. At age 60, we discover they haven't been thinking of us at all. ~ Ann Landers (1918–2002)

How old would you be if you didn't know how old you was? ~ Satchel Paige (1906–1982)

But I do fear. I fear the Dark Specter may come too soon—or do I mean too late?—that I should end before I finish, or finish but not well; that I should stain Your honor, shame Your name, grieve Your loving heart. For, they tell me, few finish well....Lord, let me get home before dark. ~ J. Robertson McQuilkin

8

Take Me Home Before Dark

One dropped ball defined the entire span of Mickey Owen's eighty-nine years of life according to his obituary in *The State*, July 16, 2005. This infamous dropped third strike occurred in the 1941 World Series when the team on which he played, the Brooklyn Dodgers, played the New York Yankees. Brooklyn had a 4-3 lead in Game 4 with two outs in the last inning when Owen dropped the third strike to Tommy Henrich. The passed ball gave the Yankee's new life which led to their winning the game by scoring four runs.

It is interesting to note little was said about Owen's hitting the first home run as a pinch hitter in an All Star game in 1942 or the fact that he made four All Star teams. The whole of his life, according to the obituary, was defined by one dropped ball.

How would you like your life to be defined by one dropped ball? Sadly, our life's successes can be clouded with one failure. David's great accomplishments for God in being king and in writing many of the Psalms are overshadowed by his one dropped ball with Bathsheba. Samson's successes for God are overshadowed by his dropped ball regarding Delilah. John Mark's successes for God are overshadowed by his dropped ball in deserting Paul at Pamphylia. Peter's great accomplishments for the Kingdom of God are overshadowed by his dropped ball in Caiaphas' palace.

As with these, so it is even with us that one dropped ball, one flagrant sin, can cast a cloud over all our many spiritual successes and achievements. Unfair, yes, but nonetheless that's how it is. One sin may color all of life.

Vance Havner at age 79 in the sermon "Home Before Dark" said, "Lord, I'd like to get Home before I make some big blunder along the way. I'd like to get Home before dark."

Aging Honorably and Happily

Old age is not the time to let one's guard down. Stay vigilant and alert, for the Devil our adversary is as a roaring lion seeking whom he may devour. Temptations thought long past coming have a way of reappearing in the senior years (I Corinthians 10:12). Determine not to allow a last inning blunder to soil your reputation, diminish your influence, destroy your ministry and shipwreck your soul.

I don't know about you, but I join Vance Havner in saying, "Lord, take me Home before dark!"

Just for laughs:

As a young pastor I asked an elderly saint how she was doing one morning, and she replied, "Brother Frank, I'm not doing well. I slept with the 'ritis' brothers last night." I was taken back, for I knew she was a widow. She then clarified, "I slept with Arthur and Bert (arthritis and bursitis.)"

Last year I replaced all the windows in my house with the expensive, double-paned, energy-efficient kind. But today I got a call from the contractor complaining that his work had been completed a whole year and I had yet to pay for them.

Boy, oh boy, did we go around! Just because I'm blonde doesn't mean that I am automatically stupid. So I proceeded to tell him just what his fast-talking sales guy had told me last year. He said that in one year the windows would pay for themselves. There was silence on the other end of the line, so I just hung up, and he hasn't called back. I guess he was embarrassed.[85]

True love isn't Romeo and Juliet who died together. It's Grandma and Grandpa who grew old together. ~ Unknown

Grow old along with me! The best is yet to be, the last of life, for which the first was made. Our times are in His hand who saith, 'A whole I planned; youth shows but half. Trust God; see all, nor be afraid![86] ~ Robert Browning

When we get to the end of our lives together, the house we had, the cars we drove, the things we possessed won't matter. What will matter is that I had you and you had me.[87] ~ Anonymous

9

Growing Old Together

The late British Prime Minister Winston Churchill, who helped defeat Hitler and save the Free World, said, "My biggest achievement was persuading my wife to marry me." Husbands, do I hear you saying a big "Amen" in agreement to that regarding your wife?

Dr. James Dobson encapsulates better than anyone what both husband and wife need from each other as they move into the latter decades of their life together.

"In conclusion, let's return to the relationship between men and women as it pertains to the process of aging. What does a woman most want from her husband in the fifth, sixth, and seventh decades of her life? She wants and needs the same assurance of love and respect that she desired when she was younger. This is the beauty of committed love—that which is avowed to be a lifelong devotion. A man and woman can face the good and bad times together as friends and allies. By contrast, the youthful advocate of 'sexual freedom' and noninvolvement will enter the latter years of life with nothing to remember but a series of exploitations and broken relationships. That short-range philosophy which gets so much publicity today has a predictable dead end down the road. Committed love is expensive, I admit, but it yields the highest returns on the investment at maturity."[88]

A Ruth kind of relationship commitment

The husband and sons of Naomi died, prompting her departure back to Bethlehem. "So Naomi and her daughters-in-law got ready to leave Moab to return to her homeland. With her two daughters-in-law she set out from the place where she had been living, and they took the road that would lead them back to Judah. But on the way, Naomi said to her two daughters-in-law, 'Go back to your mothers' homes. And may the LORD reward you for your kindness to your husbands and to me. May the LORD bless you with the security of another marriage.' Then she kissed them good-bye, and they all broke down and wept" (Ruth 1:6–9 NLT).

Orpah returned to Moab, but Ruth with unswerving commitment said, "Do not urge me to leave you or to return from following you. For where you go I will go, and where you lodge I will lodge. Your people shall be my people, and your God my God. Where you die I will die, and there will I be buried. May the LORD do so to me and more also if anything but death parts me from you" (Ruth 1:16–17 ESV).

Max Lucado in writing of Ruth's devotion, love and faithfulness to Naomi states, "One relationship of this caliber can buoy us through the fiercest storms. It was the Beatles who sang, 'Will you still need me, will you still feed me, when I'm sixty-four?'

"Oh, the agony of being sixty-four (or any age for that matter) and having no one care for you or need you. Every person is in need of at least one faithful friend or a mate who will look him or her in the eye and say, 'I will never leave you. You may grow old and gray, but I will never leave you. Your face may wrinkle, and your body may ruin, but I will never leave you. The years may be cruel, and the times may be hard, but I will never leave you."[89]

The Scottish author, poet, and Christian minister George MacDonald states, "To be trusted is a greater compliment than being loved."[90] Well put. Our life's mate must have every reason to trust our faithfulness and dependability to her or him regardless of the season in life.

Steven Curtis Chapman, in the song *I Will Be Here,* pictures the trust that must be engendered in one's husband or wife. Here's the backdrop to its writing.

Wanting to assure his wife, Mary Beth, that their marriage

Growing Old Together

wouldn't crumble as his parents' had, Chapman wrote the song. Chapman said, "It felt like I needed to drive a stake in the ground again and say to her, 'No matter how I feel when I wake up tomorrow, no matter how disillusioned we may be at different points of this, I have made this commitment to you, and I will be here when you wake up.' Because I think there was this real fear in her that said, 'Wow, if this happened in his parents' lives, what assurance do we have that this won't be our story as well?'"[91]

Why not drive a *stake* in the ground as Chapman did for Mary Beth by sharing these words truthfully with your spouse *again*.

> I will be here, and you can cry on my shoulder
> When the mirror tells us we're older.
> I will hold you to watch you grow in beauty
> And tell you all the things you are to me.
>
> We'll be together, and I will be here.
> I will be true to the promises I've made
> To you and to the One who gave you to me.
> I will be here.

Just for Laughs

Agatha Christie wrote on one occasion that she married an archaeologist. Someone asked, "Why would you marry an archaeologist?" to which she replied, "Because the older I get the more he'll appreciate me."

A man reading the newspaper was struck behind the head by his wife with a frying pan. He asked, "What was that for?"

She said, "I found a piece of paper in your pocket with 'Betty Sue' written on it."

Aging Honorably and Happily

He replied, "Honey, I went to the track last week, and the name of the horse I bet on was 'Betty Sue.'" She shrugged her shoulders and walked away.

A week later she popped him up against the head again with a frying pan. He asked, "What was that for?"

She answered, "Your horse called."

Grandchildren are the crown of the aged. ~ Proverbs 17:6 ESV

Every time a child is born, a grandparent is born too. ~ Unknown

If I'd known grandchildren were so much fun, I'd have had them first. ~ Unknown

A grandfather is someone with silver in his hair and gold in his heart. ~ Unknown

Few things are more delightful than grandchildren fighting over your lap. ~ Doug Larson

10

The Joy of Grandparenting

Jay Kesler said, "Grandparents have always played an important role in providing stability and support for families."[92] Kesler further states that the family in ancient times had the involvement of the extended family, especially grandparents, for such was crucial to the survival of the children.[93] The same is no less true today.

Dr. Karl Pillemer, who studies aging and intergenerational relationships, underscores the importance of the relationship between children and their grandparents. He notes, "Research shows children need four to six involved, caring adults in their lives to fully develop emotionally and socially" and that "the grandparent/grandchild relationship is second in emotional importance only to the parent/child relationship."[94] So you have good reason to "spoil" the grands. By the way, grandparenting has a boomerang effect. As you invest in the grandchildren, they enhance your life emotionally and socially. The bottom line is that grandparenting is good medicine.

However, it is laden with potential conflicts with the grandparents' daughter/son or daughter-in-law/son-in-law in at least twelve regards (what is stated in the parentheses is the grandparents' possible objection).

1. Over what they eat (not enough veggies; too many burgers)

2. About correction (they get by without punishment too much)

3. About the gifts you give (when stored in a closet or exchanged at the store)

4. Over the baby's name (grandparents campaign for the name; when rejected, bitter feelings may arise and linger)

5. Regarding in whose home they will spend the holidays (can be contentious)

6. Concerning equal time (same time the other set of grand-parents get or else)

7. About whom they are allowed to date (you only want the best, certainly not who they are seeing at present, and say so)

8. What activities are allowed (protest their doing things your parents never would have allowed)

9. Their dress code (they shouldn't be seen in public wearing such attire)

10. About viewing habits (too much computer or television)

11. About going to church (they need to be in an evangelical church every Sunday)

12. When the grandchildren are not treated equally (it's unfair to give more attention to one child than the other)

Yes, as grandparents we have our own preferences about all these things (and of course we are always right!) because of our desire to see our grandchildren be happy, safe, and healthy and learn about God at an early age. BUT, we always must remember that they are not ours to rear.

Therefore, walk softly and choose carefully what to say and not say, refusing to interfere with their parental supervision and philosophy of child rearing unless asked (or physical or emotional abuse occurs). "Focus on being positive and supportive, not inva-sive, and you'll be a big hit as a grandparent."[95]

Don't fall into the competition trap and try to convince the grandchildren (and yourself) that you are the best grandparent. It is most futile and will only serve to alienate, not ingratiate. The same is true about harboring jealousy regarding the other set of grandparents.

The Joy of Grandparenting

Communication plan

Probably most grandparents prefer to communicate with their grandchildren via the phone. This works well until the grands enter the exciting years of adolescence, at which time they prefer contact via various smartphone modes (text, snapshot, email, etc.). So here's a heads-up. Get a smartphone and operating instructions to be prepared for that day (it will be here sooner than you imagine, if not already).

The Biblical Role of Grandparents

1. God wants you to be a Blessing Giver

"The memory of the righteous will be a blessing" (Prov. 10:7 NIV).

You are to so order your life spiritually and morally before the grandchildren that you are a blessing unto them now and after your death. Presently, can you say their memory of you will be a blessing? Will they remember you as a saintly person, praying person, loving person and caring person?

2. God wants you to be a Pattern Setter

"The righteous lead blameless lives; blessed are their children after them" (Proverbs 20:7 NIV).

God wants you to be a track setter for your grandchildren in living a life of devotion to Him, by a life of integrity, in faithfulness to the church, with unwavering stance on biblical teaching, in spiritual disciplines, and in your love for one another.

3. God wants you to be a Message Bearer

"Even when I am old and gray, do not forsake me, O God, till I declare your power to the next generation, your might to all who are to come" (Psalm 71:18).

Aging Honorably and Happily

Grandparents are to undergird the parents' task in the religious training of their grandchildren, ever sowing the seed of the Gospel so that at the earliest possible age they will receive God's gracious gift of salvation through faith in the Lord Jesus Christ.

A 2003 Barna research poll revealed that children ages five through thirteen have a thirty-two percent chance of being saved and that the percentage drops drastically to four percent for kids ages fourteen to eighteen. God is counting on us to bear His glorious message of salvation to our grandchildren while their hearts are receptive. Additionally, bear the message of biblical morality to them when they are old enough to hear and understand.

4. God wants you to be a Prayer Intercessor

"I exhort therefore, that, first of all, supplications, prayers, intercessions, and giving of thanks, be made for all men" (1 Timothy 2:1).

Martyn Lloyd-Jones stated, "Always respond to every impulse to pray. The impulse to pray may come when you are reading or when you are battling with a text. I would make an absolute law of this—always obey such an impulse."[96]

You can often stand in the gap for your grandchildren regarding their schooling, home life, sibling relationships, health, and outside influences—and should. God hears the prayers of the righteous and will speedily answer. Every day I pray a hedge of protection about our three grandchildren (Madison Clark, Jude, and Hudson) that Satan in no wise will be able to harm them.

Little may one realize how often the intercessory prayers of grandparents like you were the very thing that protected their grandchildren from harm until at home in Heaven.

The Joy of Grandparenting
Deepen the Bond with Grandchildren

The grandchild-grandparent relationship is most important for both parties. Therefore, earnest effort must be undertaken to develop it to the fullest potential.

Manifest unconditional love to your grandchildren

A key to keeping your grandchildren close is exhibiting more acceptance than condemnation toward them. As hard as it may be try to understand them (music, clothes, and hairstyle), never allow what they do to gauge your love for them. Yes, confront them about sin and errors in judgment, providing guidance, but never cause them to doubt your love and support. Remain a *go-to person* for them regardless what happens in their life.

Spend time with them individually

Group time with the grandchildren is wonderful, but deep bonding occurs in those one-on-one encounters (fishing, hunting, zoo or park visits, trips, ice cream shop).

Connect via the Internet or Skype

Grandchildren may live in another state or nation, prohibiting us from having time physically with them. Should this be the case, use Facetime/Skype or Marco Polo on a regular basis to maintain a close relationship.

Play with them

As they grow, the games will change and become more challenging, but such engagement will serve as a bridge builder into their heart.

Show interest in their activities

Make time to show up for their ball games, recitals, musicals, birthdays, and school presentations.

Aging Honorably and Happily

Instill memories that will last a lifetime

Stories from the past when their parents or you were children build memories they will never forget. Share teachable experiences and humorous ones alike.

Communicate the love of Jesus

Tremendous relationship bonding occurs with your grandchildren when you invest the Gospel in their lives.

Grandparents' purpose in life, if none other, is to enrich the lives of their grands spiritually, emotionally and socially. And we get to have fun doing it!

Just for laughs

Two elderly grandparents from a retirement center were sitting on a bench under a tree when one turned to the other and said, "Slim, I'm 83 years old now, and I'm just full of aches and pains. I know you're about my age. How do you feel?"

Slim said, "I feel just like a newborn baby."

"Really! Like a newborn baby?"

"Yep. No hair, no teeth, and I think I just wet my pants."[97]

I have a warm feeling after playing with my grandchildren. It's the liniment working.

If you live to be one hundred, I want to be a hundred minus one day so I never have to live a day without you.[98] ~ Unknown

A bank is a place where they lend you an umbrella in fair weather and ask for it back when it begins to rain.[99] ~ Robert Frost

Old age is just as important and meaningful a part of God's perfect will as is youth. God is every bit as interested in the old as in the young.[100] ~ J. O. Sanders

So teach us to number our days, that we may apply our hearts unto wisdom. ~ Psalm 90:12

He [the elderly] knows he cannot be a long way from his end. He feels that even in the course of nature, apart from what is called accidental death, there is no doubt but in a few more years he must stand before his God. He thinks he may be in Heaven in ten or twenty years, but how short do those ten or twenty years appear! He does not act like a man who thinks a coach [hearse] is a long way off and he may take his time, but he is like one who is about to go a journey and hears the post-horn blowing down the street and is getting ready. His one solicitude now is to examine himself whether he is in the faith.[101] ~ C. H. Spurgeon

11

The Exodus File

Old age without God—it is the picture of querulousness, discontent, fretfulness, gloom! Old age with God—it is love, joy, peace, gentleness, goodness. Old age without God—it is graphically described, in this chapter, as the overturn of all worldly pride and glory: "Bel boweth down, Nebo stoopeth"; it is the spoliation of the earthly temple, the pillage of everything that ministered to earth's ephemeral happiness. Old age with God—it can stand with the prophet, even in the midst of catastrophe and ruin and death, claiming as its own the sustaining words: "Even to your old age I am He."[102] ~ J. R. Macduff

As King Hezekiah approached death, the prophet Isaiah told him "Put your affairs together, for you are going to die" (2 Kings 20:1 NLT). We must heed the same counsel in the spiritual and physical sphere. This chapter's focus is on setting one's house in order in the physical sphere.

> Minimize the burden on your heirs by making your wishes known and having things organized, tidy and thorough.

We have little to do with when we depart earth for Heaven, but we do have a lot to do with the how of the exodus and its impact upon our family. Having information regarding personal, family and business affairs in place will certainly make our exodus easier for those we love. The data may be called "The Exodus File" and should contain tabbed folders with documents clearly labeled for easy access. The file should be given to your spouse/children.

Aging Honorably and Happily

Legal Documents

Attorney

Cite the name, phone number and address of the law firm/attorney who will handle the legal aspects of your estate.

Power of Attorney Documents

Financial durable power of attorney and medical power of attorney/health care proxy/living will legal documentation.

Last Will and Testament

Indicate both the executor and beneficiary designations and include the will or its copy in this folder. The power of attorney for one to serve as the executor of your estate in your behalf must be legally documented.

Funeral Documents

Funeral Arrangements

Include preferences with regard to officiating minister(s), music, musicians, pallbearers, funeral home and cemetery.

Funeral prepayment (purchase contract, cemetery, location and what it includes)

Burial plot acquisition (plot number, cemetery, location, purchase deed)

Obituary

Write out your obituary (view obituaries in the newspaper or speak to a funeral director for assistance) including:

Full name, including nickname
Birth date, place
Parents' full names
Siblings' full names
Spouse's name
Church (positions served/ministries engaged in)

The Exodus File

Christian testimony (brief)

Education

Designations, awards, recognitions

Military service

Employment

Places of residence

Survived by (list spouse, children, grandchildren, siblings, others)

Memorial or charitable donation name and address in lieu of flowers (if that is your desire)

It is advisable that your home address not be included unless someone will be present during the visitation and funeral service

Date/time/place of the visitation and funeral (subject to the funeral home's availability)

Notifications

Indicate people that especially should be made aware of your death and funeral (include phone number/email address) and newspapers in which the obituary should be placed.

Medical Documentation

Medical Transplant Donor

If you are an organ donor, specify the organ(s) to be donated.

Estate Documents

Insurance Policies

Insurance policies with description (insurance agent, death benefit, waiting period)

Annuity policies with explanation of details (value, monthly income, duration)

Long Term Care policies with brief details (provider, value, duration)

Automobile polices with details (payment date and amount)

Automobile titles (include actual titles)

Aging Honorably and Happily

House insurance policy (company, value, annual payment amount/renewal date)

Investment accounts

Cite financial institution, account number, agent

Real Estate

House title deed (proof of settlement, actual copy of deed)
Real Estate with details (personal or joint ownership, property deed/property location)

Banking/Savings

Bank/Saving accounts (institution, account number, branch). Include online login data (username/password)
Safe box location (key)

Computer/Cell phone assess

Cite login data (username/password)

Benefit Documentation

Veteran's benefits documentation
Social Security/Medicare documentation

Outstanding Liabilities/Creditors

List all to whom money is owed and the amount
Loans from family/friends
Loans from financial institutions
Credit cards
Medical (physician, dentist, therapist, etc.)
Business loans
Insurance companies
Utilities (electric, gas, water, sewer)
Lines of credit
Phone/cable/Internet
House mortgage

The Exodus File

Pest control

Internal Revenue Service (State/Federal)

Courtesy account (pay later) at the local store/pharmacy

Student loans

Promisor of financial help to whom/amount

Monthly/Annual financial obligations

Based upon creditors and liabilities, indicate monthly/annual payment obligation.

Automobile payment (payable date, amount and to whom)

House mortgage (payable date, amount and to whom)

House pest control (payable date, amount and to whom)

Utilities (payable date, amount and to whom)

Credit cards (payable date, amount owed and to whom) and monthly statements

Property taxes on home/automobiles/boats/etc. (paid to whom/amount and when)

Home/Cell phone (paid to whom/amount/when)

State/Federal taxes (paid to whom/amount/when)

Loans (paid to whom/amount/when)

Insurance payment (paid to whom/amount/when)

Pest control (paid to whom/amount/when)

Internet/cable/satellite television service (paid to whom/amount/when)

Car satellite radio (paid to whom/amount/when)

Student loans (account numbers/paid to whom/amount/when)

Outstanding Funds Receivables

Repayment to you for personal loans, reimbursements, over-payment, cancellation of services (from whom/amount/when)

Miscellaneous

Instruction to guardians of your children

Aging Honorably and Happily

Letter to your spouse, children, grandchildren and/or others

Revelation of any hiding places for personal money (It is possible my dad died with what he called his "fishing money" squirreled away in a hidden medicine bottle.)

Heirlooms and/or possessions special directives (guns, coins, stamps, paintings, furniture, etc.)

Statement about your salvation (testimony) for family/friends

Yes, it will take some time to develop the file, but it will speak volumes of love to your family upon your death that you cared enough for them to formulate it and to assist them in this difficult and challenging aspect of transition. Once a year (birthday, anniversary, etc.) review and update the file.

Just for Laughs

You know you are old when upon tying your shoestrings you ask yourself, "Is there anything else I need to do while I'm down here."

A traveler drove his car into a ditch deep in the country. He was fortunate that a farmer was nearby and came to help with his big strong horse named Buddy.

He hitched Buddy up to the car and yelled, "Pull, Nellie, pull!" Buddy didn't move. Then the farmer hollered, "Pull, Buster, pull!" Buddy didn't respond.

Once more the farmer commanded, "Pull, Coco, pull!" Nothing. Then the farmer nonchalantly said, "Pull, Buddy, pull!" And the horse easily dragged the car out of the ditch. The motorist was most appreciative and very curious. He asked the farmer why he called his horse by the wrong name three times. The farmer said, "Oh, Buddy is blind, and if he thought he was the only one pulling, he wouldn't even try!"[103]

Look, a time is coming—and has come—when you will be scattered, each one to his own home, and I will be left alone. Yet I am not alone, because my Father is with me. ~ John 16:32 NET

While the resurrection promises us a new and perfect life in the future, God loves us too much to leave us alone to contend with the pain, guilt and loneliness of our present life.[104] ~ Josh McDowell

Look for yourself, and you will find in the long run only hatred, loneliness, despair, rage, ruin, and decay. But look for Christ, and you will find Him, and with Him everything else thrown in.[105] ~ C. S. Lewis

Most loneliness results from insulation rather than isolation. In other words, we are lonely because we insulate ourselves, not because others isolate us.[106] ~ James Dobson

In that silent chamber of yours, there sitteth by your side One whom thou hast not seen, but whom thou lovest. In that lovely house of thine, the Lord of life and glory is a frequent Visitor. He loves to come into these desolate places that He may visit thee. Thy Friend sticks closely to thee. Thou canst not see Him, but thou mayst feel the pressure of His hands. Dost thou not hear his voice?[107] ~ C. H. Spurgeon

12

Battling Loneliness

Loneliness is not solitude. Solitude is "a life-giving practice that enriches our hearts with the powerful gifts of clarity, cleansing, and strength."[108] Jesus engaged in times of solitude (Mark 1:12; 3:7, 13).

Paul Tillich shares a helpful distinction between solitude and loneliness: "Loneliness expresses the pain of being alone, and solitude expresses the glory of being alone."[109]

Covet, crave to be alone with God. Joshua was alone with God when called to ministry (Joshua 1:1). Moses was alone when the bush burned in the wilderness (Exodus 3:1–5). Gideon was alone when God raised him up to save Israel (Judges 6:11). John the Baptist was alone in the wilderness (Matthew 3:1). John, the Beloved of the Lord, was exiled upon the Isle of Patmos when under divine inspiration he wrote the book of Revelation (1:9).

We must dare to be alone with God. Only in doing so will "the print of Heaven" be stamped upon us and "the power of God" infuse us.

Loneliness on the other hand, states Adrian Rogers, is "a painful sense of being unwanted, unneeded, uncared for, maybe even unnecessary."[110] And I add unloved. Loneliness also is a feeling of being invisible to others.

The elderly one who never receives a letter, never hears a word of encouragement, never feels the handclasp or hug of another, and never receives a visit knows the pain of loneliness.

Lord Byron described the agony and heartache of his loneliness. He said, "What is the worst of woes that wait on age? What stamps the wrinkle deeper on the brow? To view each loved one blotted from life's page and be alone on earth, as I am now."[111]

Aging Honorably and Happily

Perhaps you identify with him; if so, know there is reason to hope in God.

Psychologists inform us that man has the basic need for inclusion in community and close relationships. God wired us that way. It is when social relationships break down that the enemy enters sowing the seed of loneliness.

And loneliness brings or may bring sadness, emptiness, depression, anxiety and despair. It has a crippling impact upon us emotionally. One survey reveals that a whopping eighty percent of psychiatric patients sought help due to loneliness.[112]

The aged are often misunderstood

Their loneliness and brokenness due to the death of most if not all of their friends is not comprehended nor granted sympathy. Theirs is the buried generation, and among the buried are those by whom they were admired, appreciated, loved and even embraced dearly, and with whom they worshipped, served and fellowshipped. Their lingering grief and sorrow for their deceased spouse and friends, physical frailty and/or sickness that inhibits, fixation upon one day at a time, anxiety over making ends meet, and fear of facing the unknown all are often met with misapprehension, especially among the young.

> H. G. Wells said on his birthday, "I am 65, and I am lonely and have never found peace."

Coupled with the elderly's being often misunderstood is their being forgotten and forsaken. Children abandon them, friends desert them, society at large ignores them, the young overlook them, and employers don't want them, while others would euthanize them. How strange it is that relationships radically change simply by our growing older. Certainly not all relationships change drastically, but all will experience change to one degree or another.

In contrast to man's abandonment in our twilight years, God emphatically says, "Even to your old age I will be the same, And even to your graying years I will bear you! I have done it, and I will carry you; and I will bear you and I will deliver you" (Isaiah 46:4 NASB). In old age, weakness, sickness, isolation, confinement to a nursing home or otherwise, God will not abandon or forsake you. Always remember that as friend by friend departs, God remains, that in sunny days and sunless days, health and frailty, peace and anxiety, and joy and sorrow God remains with you. That day never comes when God abandons His child.

God promises never to leave you alone. Adrian Rogers well said, "You may be lonely, but you've never alone."[113] The Amplified Bible bases its translation of Hebrews 13:5b upon Kenneth Wuest's interpretation which states that three negatives precede the verb. It is thus rendered, "Himself has said, I will not in any way fail you nor give you up nor leave you without support. *I will not, I will not, I will not* in any degree leave you helpless nor forsake nor let you down (relax My hold on you)! Assuredly not!" Four times in this one verse God promises never to leave you alone!

But as if that promise in itself were not sufficient to prove God is ever with you, the Bible abounds with others.

"Even if my father and mother abandon me, the LORD will hold me close" (Psalm 27:10 NLT).

"And the LORD, he it is that doth go before thee; he will be with thee, he will not fail thee, neither forsake thee: fear not, neither be dismayed" (Deuteronomy 31:8).

"Fear thou not; for I am with thee: be not dismayed; for I am thy God: I will strengthen thee; yea, I will help thee; yea, I will

Aging Honorably and Happily

uphold thee with the right hand of my righteousness" (Isaiah 41:10).

"And even when I am old and gray, O God, do not forsake me, until I declare Your strength to this generation, Your power to all who are to come" (Psalm 71:18 NASB).

I've seen the lightning flashing
 And heard the thunder roll;
I've felt sin's breakers dashing,
 Trying to conquer my soul.
I've heard the voice of my Savior
 Telling me still to fight on;
He promised never to leave me,
 Never to leave me alone.

The world's fierce winds are blowing;
 Temptation's sharp and keen.
I have a peace in knowing
 My Savior stands between.
He stands to shield me from danger
 When earthly friends are gone;
He promised never to leave me,
 Never to leave me alone.

When in affliction's valley
 I'm treading the road of care,
My Savior helps me to carry
 My cross when heavy to bear.
Though all around me is darkness,
 Earthly joys all flown,
My Savior whispers His promise,
 "I never will leave thee alone."

Battling Loneliness

He died for me on the mountain;
    For me they pierced His side.
For me He opened the fountain,
    The crimson, cleansing tide.
For me He's waiting in glory,
    Seated upon His throne;
He promised never to leave me,
    Never to leave me alone.

No, never alone,
No, never alone,
He promised never to leave me,
Never to leave me alone. ~ Unknown

Jesus understands loneliness

He experienced the ultimate pain of loneliness upon the Cross when making possible man's salvation from sin. The Bible states Jesus cried, "Eli, Eli, lama sabachthani?" that is, "My God, My God, why hast thou forsaken me?" about the ninth hour (Matthew 27:46). John MacArthur states "The Father for-sook the Son because the Son took upon Himself 'our trans-gressions,...our iniquities'" (Isaiah 53:5).[114]

The disciples also forsook Him along with the crowd gath-ered at the cross. Jesus died alone. But in His loneliness, He rested upon God's promises and won the day.

So Jesus has empathy with the lonely and is able to bring healing to their wounded soul. He cares for you. He loves you. He stands ready to help you.

No one ever cared for me like Jesus;
    There's no other friend so kind as He.
No one else could take the sin and darkness from me;
    Oh, how much He cared for me! ~ Charles Weigle

Aging Honorably and Happily

In order to know the healing of loneliness, you must know its Healer personally. As long as you remain outside the family of God, loneliness will be inescapable.

Just for Laughs

It is said that there are only three stages in life: youth, adulthood, and "My, you're looking well." And when they start saying that to you, you know where you are.

A woman brought a very limp duck to a veterinary surgeon. As she laid her pet on the table, the vet pulled out his stethoscope and listened to the bird's chest.

After a moment or two, the vet shook his head and sadly said, "I'm sorry; your duck, Cuddles, has passed away."

The distressed woman wailed, "Are you sure?"

"Yes, I am sure. Your duck is dead," replied the vet.

"How can you be so sure?" she protested. "I mean you haven't done any testing on him or anything. He might just be in a coma or something."

The vet rolled his eyes, turned around and left the room. He returned a few minutes later with a black Labrador retriever. As the duck's owner looked on in amazement, the dog stood on his hind legs, put his front paws on the examina-tion table, and sniffed the duck from top to bottom. He then looked up at the vet with sad eyes and shook his head.

The vet patted the dog on the head and took it out of the room. A few minutes later he returned with a cat. The cat jumped on the table and also delicately sniffed the bird from head to foot. The cat sat back on its haunches, shook its head, meowed softly and strolled out of the room.

Battling Loneliness

The vet looked at the woman and said, "I'm sorry, but as I said, this is most definitely, one hundred percent certifiably a dead duck."

The vet turned to his computer terminal, hit a few keys and produced a bill, which he handed to the woman. The duck's owner, still in shock, took the bill. "$150!" she cried. "$150 just to tell me my duck is dead!"

The vet shrugged, "I'm sorry. If you had just taken my word for it, the bill would have been $20, but with the *Lab Report* and the *Cat Scan*, it's now $150."[115]

Let your hope of heaven master your fear of death.[116] ~ William Gurnall

One of the greatest gifts we can give people is the hope that their death is nothing to fear—you know, not that it has no fear in it, but the promise of Scripture is that God will lead us through the valley of the shadow of death.[117] ~ Max Lucado

When I tread the verge of Jordan,
    Bid my anxious fears subside;
Death of deaths and Hell's destruction,
    Land me safe on Canaan's side. ~ William Williams
                    ("Guide Me, O Thou Great Jehovah")

To overcome the fear of death, we must look to Jesus Christ on the cross atoning for us, in the resurrection rising for us, in the Glory taking possession of our Home for us, and at the right hand of God preparing our place for us, possessing all power and using it so that He may bring us unto His eternal Kingdom—and soon to come again, in all the glory of the latter days, to raise the bodies of His people from the dead unless they are still alive at His coming. This is He who conquers for us the fear of death! It is to Him we are to look—"looking unto Jesus." Let your eyes be always looking to Him—then the fear of death will not make you subject to bondage.[118] ~ C. H. Spurgeon

13

No Need to Fear the Crossing of Jordan (Death)

T. DeWitt Talmage in the sermon "The Ferry-Boat of the Jordan" (2 Samuel 19:18) likens the believer's departure from earth to Heaven to that of the transportation of David and his family from one side of the river Jordan to the other. Aptly he states that the ferry boat had to be sent from the other side by the tribe of Judah. Praise God, there is a ferry-boat God is sending from the other side named mercy, grace and salvation for the redeemed. Man-made Heavenbound vessels on this side will shipwreck in the journey (morality, self-righteousness, ordinances, religious piety).

Note that the King along with his household were aboard the ferry. The presence of the King aboard assured the passengers that the utmost precautions had been taken to insure safe travel.

Talmage states, "When a soul goes to Heaven, it does not go alone. The King is on board the boat. Was Paul alone in the last exigency? Hear the shout of the scarred missionary as he cries out, 'I am now ready to be offered, and the time of my departure is at hand.'

"Was John Wesley alone in the last exigency? No. Hear him say, 'Best of all, God is with us.' Here is the promise: 'When thou passest through the waters, I will be with thee, and through the rivers, they shall not overflow thee.' Christ at the sick pillow to take the soul out of the body; Christ to help the soul down the bank into the boat; Christ midstream; Christ on the other side to help the soul up the beach!

Be comforted about your departed friends. Be comforted about your own demise when the time shall come. Tell it to all the people under the sun that no Christian ever dies alone. The King is in the boat."[119]

Aging Honorably and Happily

Knowing not only that the King has sent a ferry for our exodus into the next world but that He is aboard should calm our fears, cease our trembling, and marshal confident assurance that the trip will be successful. The saint with this knowledge can shout to death, "O death, where is your victory? O death, where is your sting? For sin is the sting that results in death, and the law gives sin its power. But thank God! He gives us victory over sin and death through our Lord Jesus Christ." (I Corinthians 15:55–57, NLT).

Billy Graham on Going Home

"How can we ever begin to know," writes Billy Graham, "the rejoicing that will take place when the Lord brings all of us home in immortal bodies? The morning stars will sing together, and the angels will shout for glory. Think of having complete fulfillment, knowing that our homecoming brings unspeakable joy to our wonderful Lord! So why do we prefer lingering here? Because we are not only earthbound in body; we are earthbound in our thinking. But when we leave this place, we will never dwell on it again. Our eyes and hearts will be fixed on Christ."[120]

D. L. Moody's Fear of Death

The famous evangelist Dwight L. Moody said, "When it comes to death, some men say, 'I do not fear it.' I feared it and felt terribly afraid when I thought of being launched into eternity to go to an unknown world. I used to have dreadful thoughts of God, but they are all gone now. Death has lost its sting. And as I go on through the world I can shout now when the bell is tolling, 'O death, where is thy sting?' And I hear a voice come rolling down from Calvary: 'Buried in the bosom of the Son of God.' He robbed death of its sting; He took away the sting of death when He gave His own bosom to the stroke."[121]

"What an argument for the truth of religion," states Albert Barnes, "what an illustration of its sustaining power, what a

No Need to Fear the Crossing of Jordan (Death)

source of comfort to those who are about to die to reflect that religion does not leave the believer when he most needs its support and consolation; that it can sustain us in the severest trial of our condition here; that it can illuminate what seems to us of all places most dark, cheerless, dismal, repulsive—'the valley of the shadow of death.'"[122]

A boy highly allergic to bee stings riding in the car with his father became terrified when a bee flew in the window. The father stopped the car, allowing the boy to get out while he caught the bee. Back in the car, the boy both saw the bee and heard it buzzing and cried out with fear once again. The boy's fear was calmed when the father simply opened his hand revealing the bee's stinger. Death makes a lot of fuss and noise but is powerless to harm us, for Jesus Christ bore its stinger upon the Cross.

A father's business required him to take a long walk through the Alps early in the morning and back home after dark. As his son grew up, he begged to be taken on these trips, but the father thought his little legs too weak to make the journey.

Finally, after years of refusal the father gave in and agreed to take him on the next trip. In the early morning walk they crossed a high rope bridge with a few missing slats suspended over the valley. With daylight and dad leading the way it posed no problem for the young boy to cross.

Once completing their business in the city they set out for home. The boy began to worry about crossing the rope bridge at dark and shared that fear with his father. The missing slats, the deep gorge, the thick darkness all were of grave concern. Unable to cross the bridge until they came to it, the father was unable to give the boy assurance everything would be just fine. With strong arms and a loving heart he placed his son on his back seeking to assure him.

Aging Honorably and Happily

The next thing the boy remembered was awaking to early rays of sunlight and seeing a silhouette of his father standing in the doorway. "Dad, what happened?" the boy inquired. "What about the bridge?" he worried out loud.

"Well, son, you fell asleep with your arms around my neck. I carried you across the bridge and laid you safely in your own bed. You've just awakened on the other side."[123] What a beautiful picture of the death of a child of God!

> Of course. Of course. ~ C. S. Lewis (referring to the first words the believer will say in Heaven)

It is said that when Stonewall Jackson lay dying he said, "Let us cross over the river and rest under the shade of the trees." One day the Christian will cross over chilly Jordan and set his feet upon the soil of sweet Beulah Land where he will find rest beneath the shade of the Tree of Life forever.

Matthew Henry is right in stating, "He whose head is in Heaven need not fear to put his feet into the grave."[124] Heaven is not mere speculation but a divine certainty.

What may be my future lot,
High or low, concerns me not.
This doth set my heart at rest:
What my God appoints is best. ~ Unknown

In approaching death, may your attitude and outlook be that of Lord William Russell. In walking to the place of his execution, he passed by his clergyman. He stopped, placed his watch in the hands of the minister, saying, "Sir, the timepiece is yours. I am now to live in eternity." If you know Jesus Christ as your personal Lord and Savior, this outlook shall be yours as well.

No Need to Fear the Crossing of Jordan (Death)

Just for Laughs

The Four Stages of Life:
1) You believe in Santa Claus.
2) You don't believe in Santa Claus.
3) You are Santa Claus.
4) You look like Santa Claus.

A woman shared with her friend that she felt her body had gotten totally out of shape and that her doctor gave her permission to join a fitness club. She told her that she decided to take an aerobics class for seniors. She said, "I bent, twisted, gyrated, jumped up and down, and perspired for an hour. But by the time I got my leotards on, the class was over."

Our days are numbered. One of the primary goals in our lives should be to prepare for our last day. The legacy we leave is not just in our possessions, but in the quality of our lives. What preparations should we be making now? The greatest waste in all of our earth, which cannot be recycled or reclaimed, is our waste of the time that God has given us each day. ~ Billy Graham

May divine grace cause you so to set this house in order that you may leave it without reluctance and enter into the next with joy, leaving your first house behind without shame in sure and certain hope of a blessed resurrection! May you cheerfully leave the first house and joyfully surrender the key to the Great Landlord.[125] ~ C. H. Spurgeon

You live as if you were destined to live forever. No thought of your frailty ever enters your head; of how much time has already gone by, you take no heed. You squander time as if you drew from a full and abundant supply, though all the while that day which you bestow on some person or thing is perhaps your last.[126] ~ Seneca

As sailing into port is a happier thing than the voyage, so is age happier than youth—that is, when the voyage from youth is made with Christ at the helm.[127] ~ Rev. J. Pulsford

14

Set Your House in Order

As John Newton lay on his deathbed, someone asked him, "Are you still with us?" Newton whispered, "I am still in the land of the dying, but soon I shall be in the land of the living."

All need a departure plan from this life. If not, we can be left in a dire predicament similar to that of a man stranded in the Alaskan wilderness. In the spring of 1981, this photographer was flown into the desolate north country of Alaska to explore the mysteries of the tundra. He carried with him 500 rolls of film, firearms, and 1,400 pounds of provisions. Entries in his journal revealed that first he was consumed with the wonder and awe of the wildlife and terrain, but in time they evolved into a record of a nightmare.

In August he wrote, "I think I should have used more foresight about arranging my departure. I'll soon find out." He died in November in a nameless valley by a nameless lake. Investigators discovered that although he had meticulously mapped out his exploration, he failed to make provision for his exodus.[128]

Do you have an exodus plan from this life in place? The prophet Isaiah said to Hezekiah, "Set thine house in order" (2 Kings 20:1). The prophet Amos emphasizes the same: "Prepare to meet thy God" (Amos 4:12). The injunction likewise is for us.

David told Jonathan, "There is but a step between me and death" (1 Samuel 20:3). Adrian Rogers in the sermon "Five Minutes After Death" said, "'There is but a step between me and death.' I wonder if you realize that is true. Death is only a faint heartbeat away, only a heartbeat, only a step. Put your hand up there; do you feel that little heartbeat? That's all there is between you and death, only a step."

Aging Honorably and Happily

All of us must acknowledge that Rogers is right, that the step of death is couching at our door. This step of death is a certain step. The record book attests of kings and queens that they lived, they ruled, and they died. All, regardless of power or wealth, have an appointment with death.

Though a certain step, it yet is an uncertain step, for hidden are the details of when, where and how. Death is ultimately a final step in that it seals forever man's opportunity to get right with God through His Son the Lord Jesus Christ.

It is a sad step for the unsaved for they will be ushered into an eternity in Hell to experience torment, but it is a joyous step for the saved in that they will finally be at Home with Jesus and loved ones.

Death—you can't escape it, avoid it, cheat it or buy your way out of it. You can only prepare for it. Are you ready for the step of death? You can only give an affirmative answer if you have personally turned from your sin and invited Jesus Christ into your life as Lord and Savior. You may go to Heaven without a lot of things, but you cannot go there apart from being born again. The time of preparation is now. Tomorrow may be too late. The apostle Paul stated, "Now is the accepted time; behold, now is the day of salvation." (2 Corinthians 6:2).

Jeremy Taylor declared about death, "Since a man stands perpetually at the door of eternity and, as did John the Almoner, every day is building his sepulcher, and every night one day of our life is gone and passed into the possession of death, it will concern us to take care that the door leading to Hell does not open upon us, that we are not crushed to ruin by the stones of our grave and that our death become not a consignation of us to a sad eternity."[129]

The best and only way to set your house in order in preparation for the rendezvous with death is through a personal relationship with the Lord Jesus Christ. In heartfelt sincerity and simple faith turn from your sin, asking its forgiveness, and invite Jesus Christ into your life to live as Lord and Savior (Romans 10:13). With regard to salvation I am happy to say you're not too old to be saved.

Following my sermon in Double Springs, Alabama, an old man walked the aisle. He asked, "Is it too late for an eighty-three-year-old man to be saved?" The man gloriously was saved, just as you may be even now.

Lord Jesus, I am sorry for my sin and now turn from it to You for forgiveness and salvation. Come into my heart and reign as Lord and Savior forever, I pray. In the name of Him who died upon the cross and was raised from the dead to make salvation possible for all who would believe and receive it, the name of Jesus Christ, I pray. Amen.

C. H. Spurgeon said, "For a man to be unconverted at the age to which some of you have attained is indeed to have a fool's cap made of gray hairs; but if you have a heart consecrated to Christ, to be His children now, with the full belief that you shall be His forever, is to have a crown of glory upon your brows."[130] (Proverbs 16:31)

Just for laughs

A man asked a lawyer, "What is your fee?"

The lawyer said, "One thousand dollars for 3 questions."

The man replied, "Wow—so much! Isn't it a bit expensive?"

The lawyer answered, "Yes. What is your third question?"

Aging Honorably and Happily

A wife was making a breakfast of fried eggs for her husband. Suddenly her husband burst into the kitchen. "Careful," he said, "CAREFUL! Put in some more butter! Oh my gosh! You're cooking too many at once. TOO MANY! Turn them! TURN THEM NOW! We need more butter. Oh my gosh! WHERE are we going to get MORE BUTTER? They're going to STICK! Careful. CAREFUL! I said be CAREFUL! You NEVER listen to me when you're cooking! Never! Turn them! Hurry up! Are you CRAZY? Have you LOST your mind? Don't forget to salt them. You know you always forget to salt them. Use the salt. USE THE SALT! THE SALT!"

The wife stared at him. "What in the world is wrong with you? You think I don't know how to fry a couple of eggs?"

The husband calmly replied, "I just wanted to show you what it feels like when I'm driving."[131]

Even to your old age I will be the same, And even to your graying years I will bear you! I have done it, and I will carry you; And I will bear you and I will deliver you. ~ Isaiah 46:4 NASB

Plan for the golden years. You may get to experience them. ~ Unknown

Forgive and give as if it were your last opportunity. Love like there's no tomorrow, and if tomorrow comes, love again.[132]

~ Max Lucado

Shall we sit idly down and say
The night hath come; it is no longer day?
The night hath not yet come; we are not quite
Cut off from labor by the failing light.
Something remains for us to do or dare;
Even the oldest tree some fruit may bear.

~ Henry W. Longfellow

15

What Matters Most at the End?

Ira Byock in *Four Things That Matter Most,* based upon research among the terminally ill, states the four things that matter most at the end of life are saying, "I forgive you"; "Forgive me"; "Thank you"; "I love you." Certainly the elderly concur.

I forgive you. You don't forgive because people deserve forgiveness but because God out of His infinite love forgave you and tells you to do the same with those who are personally offensive. Forgive even if they don't ask to be forgiven. "Be kind and compassionate to one another, forgiving each other, just as in Christ God forgave you" (Ephesians 4:32 NIV).

Ask yourself, do you want things bitter with others or better at this stage of life? It's your choice.

Forgive me. The most difficult words to say in any language are, "I am sorry. I was wrong. Please forgive me." The horrendous pain inflicted upon others by words or actions must be acknowledged to self and admitted to them in a spirit of grave humility and godly sorrow. Benjamin Franklin well advises, "Never ruin an apology with an excuse."[133] That is, never attach a "but" to the phrase "I am sorry."

Of whom do you need to ask forgiveness? Seek them out today with heartfelt sincerity to say all nine words: "I am sorry. I was wrong. Please forgive me." Remember, hurts left unattended by those who inflict them are never fully healed in either the offender or the offended. As long as you stubbornly embrace unwillingness to request forgiveness for a wrong done, an "elephant" will always remain in the room.

Thank you. "Be ye thankful" (Colossians 3:15). Vance Havner beautifully said, "We grow up taking things for granted and saving our flowers for the dead. All along the way countless hands minister to our good, but rarely do we acknowledge them." Billy Graham said, "Gratitude is one of the greatest Christian virtues; ingratitude, one of the most vicious sins."[134] And Shakespeare stated, "Blow, blow, thou winter wind. Thou art not so unkind as man's ingratitude."[135] All of us have those who have left a huge footprint upon our life, impacting it for the far better. Don't be as the nine lepers who refused to return to say thanks to Jesus for their healing, but as the only one who did (Luke 17:11–19). Unexpectedly make someone's day by expressing gratitude to them (family members, friends, hospice workers, doctors, nurses and others who provide loving care and comfort for you in times of sickness and distress).

I love you. Certainly these words ought not to be shared indiscriminately with all, but sincerely with some. Saying "I love you" in tongue-and-cheek fashion demeans, devalues and deflates the term. Its fullest fragrance (blessing) is extracted when used sincerely, reservedly and sparingly.

To genuinely say "I love you" without adding any qualifier is easier for some than for others. If it is difficult for you, start with saying, "You matter to me," or, "I thank God for you," or, "I care for you," with the goal of eventually saying, "I love you."

Fear or reluctance in expressing love verbally, in writing and/or through gifts must be thwarted by faith and reliance upon the Lord. Max Lucado states, "There is a time for risky love. There is a time for extravagant gestures. There is a time to pour out your affections on one [ones] you love. And when the time comes, seize it; don't miss it."[136]

When and to whom have you last said, "I love you?" To whom are the words overdue (spouse, child, sibling, friend)? Picture the smiling faces of people you deeply love and appreciate, knowing they will not always be around for you to express that

What Matters Most at the End?

love and affection to. In the event of death (yours or theirs) you will not regret having told them you love them, but you will regret not having told them.

When friends become strangers

Over time strangers may become friends, but also friends may become strangers unless the relationship is cultivated. In the final quarter of life one needs especially to work hard at maintaining abiding friendships.

Restore the closeness and affinity with the most important people in your life by saying the most important things while it's possible to do so. Don't wait until their eulogy or after their departure to share the treasure and blessing they are to you. Say it when it counts the most—now.

A little more tired at close of day,
A little less anxious to have our way,
A little less ready to scold and blame,
A little more care of a brother's name,
And so we are nearing the journey's end,
Where time and eternity meet and blend.

A little more love for the friends of youth,
A little less zeal for established truth,
A little more charity in our views,
A little less thirst for the daily news,
And so we are folding our tents away
And passing in silence at close of day.

A little less care for the bonds and gold,
A little more zest in the days of old,
A broader view and a saner mind,
A little more love for all mankind,
And so we are faring down the way
That leads to the gates of a better day. ~ Author Unknown

Aging Honorably and Happily

Just for laughs

Senior citizens have begun texting with their own vocabulary:

BFF: Best Friend Fainted
BYOT: Bring Your Own Teeth
CBM: Covered by Medicare
FWB: Friend with Beta-blockers
LMDO: Laughing My Dentures Out
GGPBL: Gotta Go, Pacemaker Battery Low!

[From a church bulletin] Ladies, don't forget the church rummage sale. It's a chance to get rid of those things not worth keeping around the house. Don't forget your husbands.

Grief may be called a life-shaking sorrow over loss. Grief tears life to shreds; it shakes one from top to bottom. It pulls him loose; he comes apart at the seams. Grief is truly nothing less than a life-shattering loss.[137] ~ Jay Adams

When you lose someone who is close to you, you don't get over it like people want you to.[138] ~ Greg Laurie

Recovery is not a process we can will but consists of experiencing many small deaths, the passing of significant anniversaries, until our identity is solid and natural is the pronoun "I."[139] ~ Mary Jane Moffat

I think I am beginning to understand why grief feels like suspense. It comes from the frustration of so many impulses that had become habitual. Thought after thought, feeling after feeling, action after action had Helen for their object. Now their target is gone. I keep on through habit fitting an arrow to the string; then I remember and have to lay the bow down. So many roads led through to Helen, I set out on one of them. But now there's an impassable frontier post across it. So many roads once; now so many culs-de-sac.[140] ~ C. S. Lewis

If I can stop one heart from breaking, I shall not live in vain.[141] ~ Emily Dickinson

Grief fills the room up of my absent child,
Lies in his bed, walks up and down with me,
Puts on his pretty look, repeats his words,
Remembers me of his gracious parts,
Stuffs out his vacant garments with his form.[142]
~ William Shakespeare, *King John*

16

When Your Spouse Dies—Living in an Empty House

Eighty percent of women will eventually live life as a widow. A husband may do great preparing his wife financially for his death, but there is no way for him to prepare her emotionally.

When your spouse dies, your world forever changes. You begin a journey that at the outset will be lonely, frightful and challenging. It is a journey on which you don't think you can walk or care to walk. But it must be undertaken. You must push beyond emotions of fear, disbelief, anxiety, confusion, anger, loneliness, guilt and depression to move forward with your life.

Martha Whitmore Hickman in *Healing After Loss: Daily Meditations for Working Through Grief* states, "One of the things so astonishing and costly losing a loved one is that, while the sun continues to rise and set, newspapers continue to be delivered, traffic lights still change from red to green and back again, our whole life is turned around, turned upside-down. Is it any wonder we feel disoriented and confused? Yet the people we pass on the street are going about their business as though no one's world has been shaken to the core, as though earth has not opened and swallowed us up, dropped us into a world of insecurity and change.

"It is, as Emily Dickinson says, 'a new road'—for us as surely as for the one we have lost. It will take us time to learn to walk that road. Time, and a lot of help, so we don't stumble and fall irretrievably. Those who have had their own experiences of loss will probably be our most helpful guides—knowing when to say the right word, when to be silent and walk beside us, when to reach out and take our hand. In time, we'll be helpers for others."[143]

Aging Honorably and Happily

Insights from Widows and Widowers

Much is to be learned from those whose footsteps have walked "through the valley of the shadow of death" as yours do today. I cannot identify with your grief, for I haven't loss my wife to death. But others can, due to a spouse's death, and have valuable tips to offer in how to cope with such a loss.

Vance Havner's wife's death

I couldn't put down Vance Havner's *Hope Thou in God* which to some degree chronicles his journey of grief following the death of his wife of thirty-three years, Sara. I scarcely could hold back the tears as I read of his dire loneliness, a recurring theme in the book.

Writing of Sara, he states, "Yes, the communication is cut now for a season, and I can't get through. The heart grows restless, and the wait seems long, but we have all eternity to make up for it." Then Havner exclaims to all who have experienced the death of a loved one, "We have not heard those voices, now stilled, for the last time; nor have we seen those faces finally. What the new face and voice will be like remains to be seen and heard, but our present equipment would not be able to take it if we could."[144]

C. S. Lewis' wife's death

When C. S. Lewis was asked to write a book on the problem of pain, he asked permission to write it anonymously, which was denied. In the introduction of the book *The Problem with Pain*, he writes, "If I were to say what I really thought about pain, I should be forced to make statements of such apparent fortitude that they would become ridiculous if anyone knew who made them."[145] Lewis' wife died of cancer three years after they were married causing horrendous pain and grief.

In *A Grief Observed*, Lewis shares the process of grieving he

When Your Spouse Dies—Living in an Empty House

experienced, from which the excerpt below is taken.

"No one ever told me that grief felt so like fear. I am not afraid, but the sensation is like being afraid—the same fluttering in the stomach, the same restlessness, the yawning. I keep on swallowing. At other times it feels like being mildly drunk or concussed. There is a sort of invisible blanket between the world and me. I find it hard to take in what anyone says—or perhaps hard to want to take it in. It is so uninteresting. Yet I want the others to be about me. I dread the moments when the house is empty. If only they would talk to one another and not to me."[146]

Lewis continues, "Getting over it so soon? But the words are ambiguous. To say the patient is getting over it after an operation for appendicitis is one thing; after he's had his leg off is quite another. After that operation either the wounded stump heals or the man dies. If it heals, the fierce, continuous pain will stop. Presently he'll get back his strength and be able to stump about on his wooden leg. He has 'got over it.' But he will probably have recurrent pains in the stump all his life, and perhaps pretty bad ones; and he will always be a one-legged man. There will be hardly any moment when he forgets it. Bathing, dressing, sitting down and getting up again, even lying in bed will all be different. His whole way of life will be changed. All sorts of pleasures and activities that he once took for granted will have to be simply written off—duties too. At present I am learning to get about on crutches. Perhaps I shall presently be given a wooden leg. But I shall never be a biped [two-footed] again."[147]

Lewis is correct; you will never get over it, much less get over it too soon. The death of a spouse is like an amputation of an arm or a leg which you will live without for the rest of your life. Yes, in time the pain will be less intense, adjustment will be easier, and life at large will be more manageable. But you will never get over it.

Aging Honorably and Happily

Billy Graham's wife's death

The day before Ruth's death, Billy Graham released a statement through the Billy Graham Evangelistic Association stating, "Ruth is my soul mate and best friend, and I cannot imagine living a single day without her by my side. I am more and more in love with her today than when we first met over 65 years ago as students at Wheaton College."[148]

Later Graham said, "While I will never grow accustomed to life without Ruth, she would be the first to scold me if I didn't look for God's plan for the here and now."[149]

Elisabeth Elliot's husband's death

Elisabeth and Jim had been married only twenty-seven months when he was killed by the Auca Indians. Jim was one of five missionaries killed while participating in Operation Auca, an attempt to evangelize the Huaorani people of Ecuador.

What did she do to cope with the grief over losing Jim? For sure there were none on the mission field to help her cope.

Elizabeth Elliot said, "We had been married twenty-seven months after waiting five and a half years. Five days later I knew that Jim was dead, and God's presence with me was not Jim's presence. That was a terrible fact. God's presence did not change the terrible fact that I was a widow. I expected to be a widow until I died because I thought it was a miracle I got married the first time. I couldn't imagine that I would ever get married a second, let alone a third. God's presence did not change the fact of my widowhood. Jim's absence thrust me, forced me, hurried me to God—my hope and my only refuge. And I learned in that experience who God is—who He is in a way that I could never have known otherwise."[150]

Elisabeth, speaking of the loss of Jim, states how the Lord gave her hope, peace and strength from the Holy Scriptures. Isaiah 43:2 was such a passage, the one she states kept her on the mission field and the first one that came to mind in hearing of Jim's death. "When you go through deep waters, I will be with you. When you go through rivers of difficulty, you will not drown. When you walk through the fire of oppression, you will not be burned up; the flames will not consume you (Isaiah 43:2 NLT).

She deeply felt that the Lord had called her to be a missionary prior to marriage and that the call had not been rescinded when Jim and the others were killed. After all, there was language work to be done of which she was capable. There was loss, pain and sorrow for sure, but she wouldn't have escaped it had she returned home. She remained on the field and ventured back to the very Indians who had killed her husband to win them to Jesus Christ.[151]

Elizabeth Elliot used her pain for great gain. She not only survived it but thrived in the midst of it. In knowing the everlasting arms of a loving God ever enveloped and sustained her, she was able to press forward despite the grief, loneliness, and pain.

Joyce Rogers' husband's death

In 2005 Joyce Rogers lost her husband, Adrian, of 54 years. In *Grace for the Widow* she writes with regard to his death: "I have been on this journey so I can assure you that the 'fog' will lift. The piercing ache in your heart and the flood of tears will diminish. Jesus is the healer of broken hearts. He is mending my heart as I depend upon Him. If you hand your broken heart over to Jesus, He will heal yours also. [I know where you are.] I have been there. I have longed for Adrian's arms to be around me and seek his counsel in difficult issues that have come since he passed away. I have said to myself, *If only I had someone to tell me what to do next!* I have cried out to God when I went to bed alone at night, 'Help me; help me!' And He did."[152]

Aging Honorably and Happily

"I have been in the grocery store and wondered, *What do I buy now*? Before I always thought of what Adrian would want. I am learning to say, 'Thank you for the memories.' I'm asking the question, 'Who am I now that Adrian is gone?' I'm looking to Jesus for help for today and hope for tomorrow. I can assure you that He is more than sufficient to meet all your needs. I've been to the grave, and I know he isn't there. I know that I should remember, that I shouldn't linger. I'm learning to take the journey one step at a time, leaning hard on Jesus. I'm learning to let Him fight my battles for me. Yes, the 'fog' will lift as it has for me. But life isn't easy. It will always be lived depending upon my Guide, the Lord Jesus Christ. I commend Him to you. If you hold on to His hand, He will lead you through the 'fog.'[153]

"[And until] the fog lifts, don't try to think about what your future holds. Get out of bed, take a bath, get dressed, spend time alone with God, eat breakfast, clean up the house, walk the dog, pay the bills that are due—just do the next thing. Of course, pray all through the day."[154]

Coping with the grief

How might you handle the horrendous grief? How can you live with the grief in a way that is healthy for you and others and also honors God?

Trust God even when you don't feel His presence

Jim Garlow's wife's death shook him to the core in his faith. He states, "Along the way, well-meaning people would say, 'I am sure you are feeling the presence of God.' I finally decided that I needed to be honest. Thus I answered, 'While I intellectually know He is present, I do not feel Him—at all. In my present emotional state, I am so consumed with Carol's absence that I cannot feel His presence!'"[155] As Garlow did, in the absence of feeling God's presence, faith it until you once again can feel it. He is with you whether or not you "feel" He is.

When Your Spouse Dies—Living in an Empty House

Cry

Dr. Carl Menninger states, "Weeping is perhaps the most human and universal of all relief measures."

Focus on the meaning of death

W. A. Criswell in his own exquisite and beautiful way explains death. He said, "We're to look upon that [death] in the same way as we stand and see an architect pull down an old, tottering house in order to build a better one. And there he takes off the roof, and he takes down the doors, and he pulls down the house. But first, he sends out the occupant, and after the occupant is gone, the old house is pulled down, and there he builds a new and a more glorious and a more beautiful home for the occupant.

"That's what Paul said when he said, 'Brethren, this I say, flesh and blood cannot inherit the kingdom of God' (1 Corinthians 15:50). While I'm in this house, I can't have my new house. God has to tear down this old house first before He can construct my new house, the one made without hands, eternal in the heavens [2 Corinthians 5:1]. We shall plant in the earth this house of clay, dust and ashes; God shall raise it up immortalized, glorified: 'When this mortal shall have put on immortality and when this corruptible shall have put on incorruption' [1 Corinthians 15:53].

"When I see the fallen form of the aged—there lies my father; here lies my mother; here lies my aged friend—I am not to see the old house torn down, but I am to see, by faith, the new house, the better house made without hands, eternal in the heavens [2 Corinthians 5:1]."[156]

Loosen your grip on grief

Martha Whitmore Hickman in *Healing After Loss: Daily Meditations for Working Through Grief* states, "Sometimes we're unconsciously fearful that if we begin to move away from our grief, we'll lose what contact we have with the one we miss so much....Perhaps the relinquishing of our most intense grief makes a space into which a new relationship with the loved one can move. It's the person, after all, whom we want, not the grief. May I hold my grief lightly in my hand so it can lift away from me. My connection to the one I've lost is inviolate; it cannot be broken."[157]

Time is not the healer

"You don't heal," states Carol Crandall, "from the loss of a loved one because time passes you; you heal because of what you do with the time.[158] Absorb Holy Scripture through meditation and memorization (focus upon texts that speak of God's promises to comfort and help). Engage in personal and corporate worship of God (adoration, exaltation, supplication, thanksgiving, and confession). Interact with others, drawing support. Resume responsibilities (decision making, work, school, church). Get back to your familiar routine as much as possible and as soon as possible. Rest sufficiently and eat healthily to cope with grief properly. Avoid isolation (not solitude). Grab hold of God; gaze upon God; glorify God (overrule emotions that protest).

Phillips Brooks in a letter to a friend following his mother's death said, "People bring us well-meant but miserable consolations when they tell us what time will do to help our grief. We do not want to lose our grief, because our grief is bound up with our love, and we could not cease to mourn without being robbed of our affections."[159]

Prepare for grief triggers

Watch and prepare for "grief triggers," such as Christmas, Thanksgiving, Easter, birthdays, and the anniversary of your loved one's death, which will wallop you with sadness. I experience them with regard to my parents; all will with regard to their deceased loved ones. It is natural. Have a plan in place that will lessen their impact.

When Your Spouse Dies—Living in an Empty House

Don't compare your experience with that of others

Don't compare the grieving experience of others with your own. Don't fall into the trap of allowing the grieving experiences of others to dictate how you are to respond to grief. Each person is unique and will grieve differently.

Accept your spouse's death

Accepting your wife's/husband's death is not forgetting her or him. You will never do that. Pressing forward is not saying you are over your spouse's death. That will never happen.

Jim Garlow states, "On day 100 after Carol's passing, I sat down and wrote the words, 'She is not coming back.' Up until then, I had an internal war. I simply could not let her go! I could not face life without Carol, the love of my life for the past 43 years. But on day 100, as I wrote, 'She is not coming back,' the war within me ended or at least greatly subsided. I finally allowed her to die. It was extremely painful. But it was a necessary step in order to let her die. I had to let go.

I did not experience much change initially. But at day 120 (one-third of a year), I could begin to tell a difference. Healing began. I could finally conceive of surviving. I could finally envision a future."[160]

If I should die and leave you here awhile,
Be not like others, sore, undone, who keep
Long vigil by the silent dust and weep.
For my sake turn again to life and smile,
Nerving thy heart and trembling hand to do
That which will comfort other souls than thine.
Complete these dear unfinished tasks of mine,
And I perchance may therein comfort you.
~ Mary Hall

Aging Honorably and Happily

The Sea of Nothingness and Unfamiliarity

Gerald Sittser, following the tragic death of his mother, wife and young daughter in an auto accident, wrote in *A Grace Disguised*, "Prepare for a journey on the 'Sea of Nothingness.' There are so many details to deal with in the immediate moments after the death of your spouse. Much of this activity will seem void of any sort of meaning for you. That's okay. It still needs to be done—just give yourself permission to not make more of it than you should."[161] Sittser continues, "'Say goodbye to your 'Familiar Self.' There is no more 'business as usual' once your spouse dies. The comfortable and familiar are neither anymore. Take the good memories with you and prepare to move on. God has many incredible things yet to show you. Trust Him to comfort and guide you on this new journey."[162]

Discarding of clothes and possessions

Wait until you are ready to discard the clothes and possessions of your spouse. No hurry. Don't allow others to hurry you in dealing with that matter as well as others in the grieving process.

Express your grief openly

"In some areas of Christianity," states Ron Dunn, "silence is considered to be the proper response to suffering. But silence only deepens the darkness....Suffering has an isolating effect on the sufferer. He sees himself forsaken by God and forgotten by everyone else. To remain silent under the burden of suffering means to become more and more isolated. [It] is right and essential to express the pain of our souls. Sometimes the suffering can be endured only when the pain can be articulated."[163]

Allow yourself to speak of the cause of your spouse's death, memories of his/her life, and the emotional roller coaster upon which you ride. Talk freely of your loneliness, hurt, anger, fear and uncertainty.

When Your Spouse Dies—Living in an Empty House

"Words that express your grief," John Woodhouse wrote, "will speak predominantly of the good that we have lost. That is why we are grieving. Such words are appropriate and should be understood for what they are, not criticized because they overlook weaknesses, flaws and failures. Putting our grief into words helps us understand our sadness by helping us see its cause—the good we have lost—and thank God for the goodness, because it was His gift to us."[164]

Cling to your friends

You need friends who primarily will reach out to you with a gentle, loving touch or a hug, who will allow their spirit and yours to communicate without the use of words. Charlie Walton, in his book *When There Are No Words,* explains the power of a hug in the hour of grief.

"Pain doesn't come in pounds or ounces or gallons. You just feel like you are standing before a mountain that you are going to have to move one spoonful at a time. It is a task you can never hope to complete...a mountain that you can never hope to finish moving. But...as you stand surveying that mountain of grief...a loved one steps forward with a hug that communicates clearly. You can almost picture that person stepping up to your mountain of grief with a shovel and saying, 'I cannot move the mountain for you...but I will take this one shovelful of your grief and deal with it myself.'"[165] Walton continues, "Every hug helps dilute the pain...to move the mountain. Don't be selfish with your mountain. Don't be a martyr about your grief. There is plenty of mountain to keep you busy the rest of your life...and...if your friends hadn't been willing to help...they wouldn't have showed up with those spoons, shovels and hugs."[166]

Seek professional help

Most grief, at least acute grief, will go away for most people within six months to three years of the death of their spouse. A spouse who struggles with acute grief beyond that time frame probably is experiencing "complicated grief" which will require counseling from a Christian therapist or psychologist. If this is you, don't hesitate to seek help. In times of physical hurt we seek out doctors. In times of emotional hurt we need to seek out therapists or psychologists.

Stay in church

Keep on working despite the tears of broken-heartedness. Keep teaching that church class, singing in the choir, going soul winning, working with the children/student ministry, preaching, singing despite the tears, and in doing so find comfort and healing. Don't desert the ministry God has called you to perform during your grief, no matter how difficult it is. Keep pressing on in His strength and by His grace. Within the walls of the church you will find comfort, encouragement, strength and support.

Look forward to a heavenly reunion

Charles Dickens correctly wrote, "And can it be that in a world so full and busy, the loss of one weak creature makes a void in any heart so wide and deep that nothing but the width and depth of eternity can fill it up!"[167]

Charles and Susannah Spurgeon had been married thirty-six years when Charles died in 1892. Susannah wrote, "For though God has seen fit to call my beloved up to higher service, He has left me the consolation of still loving him with all my heart and believing that our love shall be perfected when we meet in that blessed land where Love reigns supreme and eternal."[168] You and your husband/wife will meet again in Heaven. Death has but momentarily silenced the conversations and companionship.

Breaking through the barrier of sorrow

By God's grace you will break through the barrier of sorrow and be able to "breathe again." C. S. Lewis did. He says, "Something quite unexpected has happened. It came this morning early. For various reasons, not in themselves at all mysterious, my heart was lighter than it had been for many weeks....And suddenly, at the very moment when so far I mourned Helen least, I remembered her best. Indeed, it was something (almost) better than memory—an instantaneous, unanswerable impression. To say it was like a meeting would be going too far. Yet there was that in it which tempts one to use those words. It was as though the lifting of the sorrow removed a barrier."[169]

An old Chinese proverb states, "The man who removed mountains began by carrying away small stones." In rebuilding your life, just pick up one *small stone at a time*, at your own pace. What is essential in grief recovery is not how many stones are picked up quickly but that they are continuously picked up (one small stone after another) throughout the grief process.

Just for laughs

A man was talking to the family doctor. "Doc, I think my wife's going deaf."

The doctor answered, "Well, here's something you can try on her to test her hearing. Stand some distance away from her and ask her a question. If she doesn't answer, move a little closer and ask again. Keep repeating this until she answers. Then you'll be able to tell just how hard of hearing she really is."

The man went home and tried it out. He walked in the door and said, "Honey, what's for dinner?" He didn't hear an answer, so he moved closer to her. "Honey, what's for dinner?" Still no answer. He repeated this several times, until he was standing just a few feet away from her.

Finally she answered, "For the eleventh time, I said we're having MEAT LOAF!"[170]

Aging Honorably and Happily

At sixty, you've entered the "Stone Age"—gall, kidney and bladder—and your idea of weightlifting is standing up.

What a wonderful God we have—he is the Father of our Lord Jesus Christ, the source of every mercy, and the One who so wonderfully comforts and strengthens us in our hardships and trials. ~ 2 Corinthians 1:3–4.

When your spouse is diagnosed with a chronic illness, you begin to realize that your life, your spouse's life and your marriage will never again be the same.[171] ~ Erin Prater

An individual doesn't get cancer; a family does.[172]
~ Terry Tempest Williams

The greatest faith is born in the hour of despair. When we can see no hope and no way out, then faith rises and brings the victory.[173] ~ Lee Robertson

As Christians, we have been given all we need in order to face down even the most frightening, unexpected and overwhelming obstacles in life.[174] ~ David Jeremiah

"Suffering should not make us bitter people," my mother once said. "It should make us better comforters." Young people need to hear this from those who have walked before them, because someday they'll be walking those same steps, but there may not be anyone following behind.[175] ~ Billy Graham

17

Facing the Chronic Illness of Your Spouse

The diagnosis of chronic illness in your spouse happened out of nowhere. You never expected it. It has shaken your world upside down. You are overwhelmed with fear, uncertainty and confusion. You now are one of the nearly half of all Americans who live their day-to-day lives with at least one chronically ill companion.

With the arrival of senile dementia, cancer, heart disease, degenerative diseases and/or others in your spouse come horrendous pain, tremendous challenges and often difficult decisions.

Things "Not to Do" as a Caregiver

Research indicates that the well spouse is often overlooked as he/she cares for the sick spouse. In a study published in the *Journal of the Royal Society of Medicine,* "Quality of Life: Impact of Chronic Illness on the Partner," the authors stated: "...the most striking research finding is a tendency for the partner's quality of life to be worse than that of the patient."[176]

In sharing some things not to do as a caregiver, I hope it will enhance your quality of life as well as that of your sick spouse.

Don't fail to talk about the chronic illness

Boston College social work professor Karen Kayser says, "If the couple is consumed with talking about the illness, that's a problem. If they never talk about it, it's also a problem. You have to find a middle ground."[177]

Don't neglect your health

To focus solely on your sick mate's health with disregard for your own is detrimental both to him/her and yourself. Take time to eat right and exercise. Rest sufficiently.

Aging Honorably and Happily

A Canadian Academy of Health Sciences report states that the health of a caregiver for a chronically ill person is impacted in various ways, including low immune systems, slow wound healing and high blood pressure.[178]

"People overestimate their abilities and underestimate their stress levels," says Madill. She advises spousal caregivers to have regular medical checkups, specifically regarding their cortisol levels.[179] "If your cortisol levels are too high," Madill states, "you're going to burn out."[180] Cortisol determines energy levels.

Remember, if you neglect your health and it falters, you will not be able to render the care your spouse requires.

Caregiver burnout warning signs

The signs include:

Withdrawal from friends, family, and other loved ones
Loss of interest in activities previously enjoyed
Feeling blue, irritable, hopeless, and helpless
Changes in appetite, weight, or both
Changes in sleep patterns
Getting sick more often
Wanting to hurt yourself or the person for whom you are caring
Emotional and physical exhaustion
Irritability[181]

Should you begin experiencing the symptoms of burnout, seek out immediate help for both your well-being and that of your spouse.

Don't feel guilty for leaving him/her occasionally.

It is important for you to get "outside" from time to time to be renewed and refreshed. Energy and strength must be replenished. Have lunch with a friend. Go to a movie. Take a walk in the park. Go shopping. And don't feel guilty in the process. Don't allow your sick spouse's isolation to mean isolation for yourself.

Facing the Chronic Illness of Your Spouse

You should feel free to socialize even if your spouse cannot. Keeping your own identity is essential.[182]

Don't bear the burden alone

Let others help. Ann Brandt says, "Watch out for the words, 'Let me know if there is anything I can do.' Don't let those folks walk away. Give them opportunities to help. Accept help."[183]

Though a green bean casserole and fried chicken meal provided by a friend cannot heal your wounded spirit or resolve the hardship, it does lessen the load so that you may focus more on coping with your spouse's care.

Look to the church for relief. Caring, capable and compassionate believers within the household of God stand ready to assist and support. Allow them to help. Keep handy a list of things friends, relatives and fellow believers can do.

Don't hesitate to ask the doctor questions

Join your sick spouse in seeing the doctor and don't be hesitant to ask questions (write them down so none slip your mind).

Psychiatrist and caregiver health researcher Peter Rabins, M.D., M.P.H., codirector of the geriatric psychiatry and neuropsychiatry division at the Johns Hopkins Hospital, underscores this point in saying, "Work together, beforehand, to create a list of questions. This gets the two of you talking about your concerns, your worries and areas where you need more information. If there's not time to discuss all of your questions, ask if a nurse or physician's assistant can help, if you can meet at another time, or if you can discuss your concerns by phone or email."[184]

Don't neglect being a part of a support group

Though God and Holy Scripture are your stay in coping, help may be found from the experience of those who have been where you are now. Inquire of your church regarding the location of a support group for spouses of the chronically ill in your area and participate in its meetings. There is much to be gained from the experiences of someone who has been down the path we now walk.

Don't neglect God or the Bible

Nourish your soul daily. Stay close to God. Read the Bible. Paul in the later years of his life, imprisoned and awaiting death, requested Timothy to bring "the books, and above all the parchments (the Word of Jesus and Word of God—William Barclay)" (2 Timothy 4:13). The request of all seniors certainly should be, "Bring me the Book," for within its pages alone is found the wellspring of comfort, hope, faith, strength, guidance and security.

Essential also to growing old gracefully, honorably and happily is the discipline of prayer and corporate worship (church) inasmuch as possible.

Trust God even when it is difficult. John Henry Newman said, "I will trust Him. Whatever, wherever I am, I can never be thrown away. If I am in sickness, my sickness may serve Him; in perplexity, my perplexity may serve Him; if I am in sorrow, my sorrow may serve Him. My sickness or perplexity or sorrow may be necessary causes of some great end which is quite beyond us. He does nothing in vain."[185]

Heed the counsel of the psalmist when he declares, "Cast thy burden upon the Lord, and he shall sustain thee: he shall never suffer the righteous to be moved" (Psalm 55:22).

In extreme physical pain, C. H. Spurgeon preached what proved to be his last sermon. Speaking of Jesus Christ, he said at its conclusion, "He is the most magnanimous of captains. There never was His like among the choicest of princes. He is always to be found in the thickest part of the battle. When the wind blows cold He always takes the bleak side of the hill. The heaviest end of the cross lies ever on His shoulders. If He bids us carry a burden, He carries it also. If there is anything that is gracious, generous, kind, and tender, yea lavish and superabundant in love, you always find it in Him."[186]

Don't neglect your spouse's spiritual needs

Watchman Nee cautioned, "Are there not many whose spiritual life is endangered by their physical condition, many who fall because of their physical weakness, many who cannot work actively for God because of the bondage of illness."[187]

Refuse to allow sickness to injure the spiritual walk of your spouse. If he is unable to read the Bible, read it to him and/or provide it via taped recording or DVD. Invite his Sunday school teacher into your home to teach the Sunday school lesson. Share recordings of the pastor's sermons and pray with him.

In focusing on the physical and mental needs of your spouse, don't neglect the most important, the spiritual.

Don't keep emotions penned up

Your world is forever different and unsettling. And it never will be the same again. Allow yourself to grieve over that which has been irretrievably lost. It's okay and healthy to release pent up emotions through crying out to God and expressing them to others.

Don't forget you are in this together

If possible, make decisions together regarding doctors and treatment. Share heartaches and challenges with your spouse, allowing him to help lift your burden. Solomon reminds us of the strength of two in facing a crisis: "Two people are better off than one, for they can help each other succeed. If one person falls, the other can reach out and help. But someone who falls alone is in real trouble. Likewise, two people lying close together can keep each other warm. But how can one be warm alone? A person standing alone can be attacked and defeated, but two can stand back-to-back and conquer. Three are even better, for a triple-braided cord is not easily broken" (Ecclesiastes 4:9–12 NLT).

The "cord of three strands" Solomon refers is you, your spouse and God. When these three are tightly intertwined, there is tremendous hope, help and harmony despite the circumstances.

Exchange tasks to lighten the burden. Assume roles your spouse no longer can, but let it be a trade-off for something you used to do that your spouse can take over. Facing and fighting the illness as a team makes it the more bearable.

Don't try to cope with everything at once

The journey will certainly be challenging, but concentrate on one day at a time, not what's down the road. Jesus reminds us of this truth in Matthew 6:34, "So don't worry about tomorrow, for tomorrow will bring its own worries. Today's trouble is enough for today" (NLT).

Don't become disconnected from your spouse

Due to the condition of your sick spouse, any physical contact, even a hug, may be painful for you to give. This physical disconnection may lead to a disconnection mentally and emotionally when he/she misinterprets your lack of physical contact.[188] Your primary cohesive bonding to your mate outside of the physical is the spiritual.

Don't lie to yourself

There is a time to be optimistic regarding the recovery of your spouse, and sadly a time to be realistic in knowing he/she will not recover. Certainly in faith pray and believe God for restoration to health, for He is a miracle working God. But should it not be God's will to raise your spouse up, accept it, refusing to tell yourself he/she is going to be all right when in fact that is not the case.

Facing the Chronic Illness of Your Spouse

Don't belittle your spouse's condition

Treat it with gravity, not as something that is a bothersome nuisance. Your spouse certainly can tell which it is with you. Remember your sick spouse misses out on doing things that you miss out doing. Express empathy, not just sympathy.

Don't be overly negative in outlook

It's okay to express negative emotions at times, but try to be positive and optimistic in your interactions with your spouse (Badr & Carmack Taylor, 2008).[189] "When husbands and wives tackle the illness together, it can be easier to keep a positive outlook (Berg 2008)."[190]

Don't overlook financial planning

Money may readily be a problem, especially if it's the bread earner of the family that is chronically ill. Couple with that the high cost of medical care and medication, and major challenges arise, including emotional strain. Seek guidance in financial planning from a Christian financial advisor whose expertise is in handling chronic medical conditions.[191]

Make adjustments to lifestyle

Instead of attempting to maintain a "business as usual" approach in lifestyle that is a struggle, adapt to a simpler way of doing things that is easier and pleasurable.[192]

Marriage, how do you "keep it together?"

Refuse to allow chronic illness to weaken the bond between your spouse and yourself.

Statistics indicate that over seventy-five percent of marriages plagued by chronic illness end in divorce.[193] Of these marriages the most likely to fail are those whose chronically ill spouse is young.[194] The Bible does not state anywhere that the severe sickness of a spouse is cause for divorce. Pat Robertson (700 Club) was wrong in stating that if a spouse had Alzheimer's then divorce is okay because it is a type of death.[195]

The marital covenant made between two people in the presence of God and assembled witnesses clearly states that they will remain married "in sickness and in health." Perhaps in the wedding ceremony you said these words glibly, never anticipating this day of chronic illness in your mate. But it is here. Assure your spouse of your inextinguishable love and undying support.

How does a marriage survive when one partner gets sick? I know it may sound too simplistic, but it survives because of love and compassion on the part of the healthy partner and God's amazing grace to cope. Obviously the marital covenant made between the two also sustains the marriage. "More than anything," states Ashley Willis, "we need to perceive this crisis of illness as an opportunity to honor our marital vow to love each other in both sickness and health. God will use this to strengthen our marriage and our faith if we don't lose hope and stay strong together."[196]

A husband coping with his wife's chronic illness said, "The sooner one learns marriage is not 50/50 but rather 100/100, the easier things will be. I didn't commit to being a husband for my wife only fifty per cent of the time. I promised I would be there whenever she needed me and not only when it suited me."[197]

Couples with one chronically ill spouse testify that the challenges such care continuously bring actually strengthen their relationship instead of weakening it, often in ways that would benefit any marriage. Love actually may flourish more strongly in such marriages.

The very fact that you have a choice to walk away from your chronically ill spouse and you don't speaks volumes regarding your love for him/her.

Facing the Chronic Illness of Your Spouse

Just for laughs

"Oh, God," sighed the wife one morning, "I'm convinced my mind is almost completely gone!"

Her husband looked up from the newspaper and commented, "I'm not surprised. You've been giving me a piece of it every day for thirty years!"[198]

Some rock stars of the sixties and seventies are revising their songs to minister to senior adults.

Herman's Hermits—"Mrs. Brown, You've Got a Lovely Walker"
The Bee Gees—"How Can You Mend a Broken Hip"
Johnny Nash—"I Can't See Clearly Now"
Paul Simon—"Fifty Ways to Lose Your Liver"
Procol Harem—"A Whiter Shade of Hair"
The Temptations—"Papa's Got a Kidney Stone"
Leslie Gore—"It's My Procedure, and I'll Cry If I Want To"

And last but NOT least...

Tony Orlando—"Knock 3 Times on the Ceiling If You Hear Me Fall"[199]

I do not want to be a grumpy old man. God threatens terrible things to those who grumble (Psalm 106:25–26). Murmuring dishonors God who promises to work all things together for our good (Romans 8:28). Complaining puts out the light of our Christian witness (Philippians 2:14–15). And a critical, anxious spirit dries up joy and peace (Philippians 4:6–7). That is not the way I want to grow old.[200] ~ John Piper

Age is rarely despised but when it is contemptible.[201] ~ Samuel Johnson

Most people can have much to do with choosing what kind of persons they will be in the older years. Beauty and power in the senior years do not just happen. They are no accidents. One in the early years largely determines what the later years are like.[202] ~ Frank Stagg

18

Avoiding Being a Grouchy Old Man or Woman

When I think of a "grouchy old man," my mind turns to Ben Weaver (grumpy, stingy, miserable and negative) on the *Andy Griffith Show*. Weaver was the proprietor of Weaver's Department Store in Mayberry and also a landlord with rental property.

Often people who are optimistic, pleasant and congenial in early life find themselves becoming like Ben Weaver in later life. Grumpiness and other expressions of crankiness seem to kick in at age sixty for these persons.

How can we ensure that we avoid the "grumpy old man" syndrome and remain positive throughout our advancing years?

Acceptance

A recent worldwide survey reveals that people in their seventies in good health were as happy and mentally healthy as twenty-year-olds.[203] Why? *Psychology Today* speculates it is partly attributable to the fact that elderly people experience less stress and responsibility. Second, "it's also about 'letting go'—learning to accept your strengths and weaknesses and letting go of unrealistic goals, attachments and aspirations."[204]—that is, plain acceptance.

An unwillingness to accept change as you grow older will erode your pleasant and gentle disposition into a grumpy and bitter one. As we grow older, all of us have to face the fact that "the old gray mare ain't what she used to be" and adapt dreams, goals, activities and pursuits accordingly.

The apostle Paul emphasizes the point of being content and adaptable to change. "I'm glad in God, far happier than you would ever guess—happy that you're again showing such strong concern for me. Not that you ever quit praying and thinking about me. You just had no chance to show it. Actually, I don't have a sense of needing anything personally. I've learned by now to be quite content whatever my circumstances. I'm just as happy with little as with much, with much as with little. I've found the recipe for being happy whether full or hungry, hands full or hands empty. Whatever I have, wherever I am, I can make it through anything in the One who makes me who I am. I don't mean that your help didn't mean a lot to me—it did. It was a beautiful thing that you came alongside me in my troubles" (Philippians 4:10–14 MSG).

Exhibit Christian hope

Maintaining an optimistic rather than a pessimistic spirit is highly beneficial. It can improve health. Researchers from the University of Illinois found in a study that optimistic people have signifcantly better blood sugar and cholesterol levels, healthier body mass indexes, and were more physically active than those who dwelt on negativity.[205] Additionally in that study Rosalba Hernandez, a professor of social work at the University of Illinois, said, "Individuals with the highest levels of optimism have twice the odds of being in ideal cardiovascular health compared to their more pessimistic counterparts."[206]

Geriatrician Carmel B. Dyer, who is director of the Division of Geriatric and Palliative Medicine at the University of Texas Medical School at Houston, said, "I've been practicing geriatric medicine for almost 20 years, and I've noticed that my patients who sort of make the best of everything, when there's lemons they make lemonade…they seem to live longer and happier lives. I think if you're more optimistic, you're more positive, you're going to do better; you're going to feel better."

Dietrich Bonhoeffer said "The essence of optimism is that it takes no account of the present, but it is a source of inspiration, of vitality and hope where others have resigned; it enables a man to hold his head high, to claim the future for himself and not to abandon it to his enemy."[207]

Avoiding Being a Grouchy Old Man or Woman

But as beneficial as optimism is, the believer has something even better. He has Christian hope founded in faith in the Person and promises of Jesus Christ.

J. I. Packer draws this contrast between optimism and Christian hope:

"Optimism hopes for the best without any guarantee of its arriving," states, "and is often no more than whistling in the dark. Christian hope, by contrast, is faith looking ahead to the fulfillment of the promises of God, as when the Anglican burial service inters the corpse 'in sure and certain hope of the resurrection to eternal life, through our Lord Jesus Christ.' Optimism is a wish without warrant; Christian hope is a certainty, guaranteed by God himself. Optimism reflects ignorance as to whether good things will ever actually come. Christian hope expresses knowledge that every day of his life, and every moment beyond it, the believer can say with truth, on the basis of God's own commitment, that the best is yet to come."[208]

Most certainly the person who knows Jesus Christ personally as Lord and Savior and embraces the Christian hope He espoused will age biblically and joyfully without fear of becoming a grouchy old man or woman. Why? Billy Graham said, "Only the forward-looking Christian remains sincerely optimistic and joyful, knowing that Christ will win in the end."[209]

Stay connected and involved

Research reveals "that staying socially active and maintaining interpersonal relationships can help you stay physically and emotionally healthy—and happy."[210] Join the senior citizens group at your church and engage in its various worship and social functions. By the way, attending religious services has not only spiritual but also physical value. A 2006 study found that regular church attendance can add 1.8 to 3.1 years to your life.[211]

Aging Honorably and Happily

Enroll in a class at the YMCA or community center (computer skills, arts and crafts, cooking, drama, swimming or gardening). Plan a regular social outing with a friend (dinner, movie, bowling, etc.). As we grow older, there is much that can no longer be done by us; still, there is yet much that can and should be.

God never intended for man to live in isolation. For every "Lone Ranger" He created at least one "Tonto." Who are your Tontos? Maintain contact with them. Engage socially with them. If your "Tonto" is deceased or has moved away, seek out a new one without delay. It's most difficult to be grumpy if you have true friends with which to enjoy life on a regular basis.

Change routine

Don't get stuck in a rut. Drive a different route to the grocery store even if it's slightly further. Order something different at the restaurant, or better still, allow the waitress or waiter select the meal. Get up earlier or later. Go to bed earlier or later. Instead of watching another rerun on television, select something new to view. Choose a different path to walk or jog. Instead of sitting in front of the TV most of the day, work as a volunteer at your church, local hospital and/or community center.

It has been said, "One reason people resist change is that they focus on what they have to give up instead of what they have to gain."[212] Try not focusing upon what you have to forgo in making a change but upon the benefit that will be derived.

Don't believe the negative stereotyping

Adults who believe that with advancing age "they become more and more useless" and "things will keep getting worse with age," etc., affect their ability to cope with old age—so states the findings of a study cited in *The Journal of Personal and Social Psychology* in 2002 by Dr. Becca Levy.[213] Dr. Levy speculated in her findings "that people with positive age stereotypes have a stronger will to live, and that this might affect their ability to adapt to the rigors of older age. Also, people with negative age stereotypes may have a heightened cardiovascular response to stress, with attendant ill health effects."[214]

Resemble a child

You have never heard of a grumpy old child, right? Children occasionally have bad moods, but they quickly pass. View life through the lenses of a child, and the tendency to be negative, critical and despondent will be a nonissue.

Criticism and grumpiness go together

Criticizing, complaining, gossiping and backbiting fuel a negative mindset. Talk positively instead of negatively of people and, inasmuch as possible, about things.

Look in the mirror

"Let's not be narrow, nasty, and negative," urges T. S. Eliot.

> Let's not be narrow, nasty, and negative. ~ T. S. Eliot

One can gradually progress into being a grouchy old person seemingly without knowing it. Therefore, occasionally examine yourself whether or not you have slipped into that state. Ask, *Am I unhappy or depressed? Am I a grumpy old man/woman? Am I a Mr. Weaver?* If so, take steps to change your outlook on life and upon others.

Don't merely exist; live these adventurous senior years to their max and make things enjoyable and pleasant to others.

Alexander Knox, who knew John Wesley in his later years, shared the following description of his demeanor and life. "So fine an old man I never saw! The happiness of his mind beamed forth in his countenance. Every look showed how fully he enjoyed 'the gay remembrance of a life well spent.' In him old age appeared delightful—like an evening without a cloud; and it was impossible to observe him without wishing frequently, *May my latter end be like this.*"[215]

Don't be a Ben Weaver or Ebenezer Scrooge whom people dislike and avoid due to their grouchy disposition. Rather, be a John Wesley and grow old pleasantly and lovely.

> Let me grow lovely, growing old—
> So many fine things do;
> Laces and ivory and gold
> And silks need not be new.
> And there is healing in old trees;
> Old streets a glamour hold.
> Why may not I, as well as these,
> Grow lovely, growing old? ~ Karle Wilson Baker

Just for laughs

Two elderly women were out driving in a large car—both had trouble seeing over the dashboard. As they were cruising along, they came to an intersection. The stoplight was red, but they just went on through. The woman in the passenger seat thought to herself, *I must be losing it; I could have sworn we just went through a red light.*

After a few more minutes they came to another intersection where the light was red, and again they went right though. This time the woman in the passenger seat was almost sure that the light had been red but was really concerned that she was losing it. She was getting nervous and decided to pay very close attention to the road and the next intersection to see what was going on.

Avoiding Being a Grouchy Old Man or Woman

At the next intersection, sure enough, the light was definitely red, and they went right through. She turned to the other woman and said, "Mildred! Did you know we just ran through three red lights in a row! You could have killed us!"

Mildred turned to her and said "Oh, am I driving?"[216]

Q: Are you a scratch player in golf?

A: I sure am—every time I hit the ball I scratch my head and wonder where it went. [217]

A person heard two old people having this conversation: "I can't stand it anymore. I never can remember what I just said!"

"Oh, really? When did this problem start?"

The person replied, "What problem?"

God's man in the center of God's will is immortal until God is finished with him.[218] ~ David Jeremiah

I want to be all used up when I die. ~ George Bernard Shaw

Old age hath yet his honor and his toil. ~ Alfred Lord Tennyson

"There is a man in thy kingdom, in whom lives the spirit of the holy God; and in the days of thy father light and intelligence and wisdom, like the knowledge of God, was found in him" (Daniel 5:11 JB).

19

Retired Daniels

Matthew Henry in his commentary on Daniel 5:11 states, "There are a great many valuable men, and such as might be made very useful, that lie long buried in obscurity, and some that have done eminent services that live to be overlooked and taken no notice of. But, whatever men are, God is not unrighteous to forget the services done to His kingdom. Daniel, being turned out of his place, lived privately and sought not any opportunity to come into notice again; yet he lived near the court and within call."[219]

Joseph Parker says, "Preachers of the Word, you will be wanted some day by Belshazzar; you were not at the beginning of the feast, but you will be there before the banqueting hall is closed; the king will not ask you to drink wine, but he will ask you to tell the secret of his pain and heal the malady of his heart. Abide your time. You are nobody now. Who cares for preachers, teachers, and men of insight while the wine goes round and the feast is unfolding its tempting luxuries?"[220]

The Christian and church at large would do well to tap the knowledge, wisdom, understanding and experience of the godly elderly. Regrettably the church often overlooks, ignores or forgets these *Daniels* to its own peril.

Until summoned, resolve to be like Daniel and "live near the court and within call," ever willing to assist Christians and the church at large. Though you are forgotten, as was Daniel, God may raise up a "Queen mother" today who remembers your devotion and duty, prompting your solicitation to help (Daniel 5:10).

Aging Honorably and Happily

Minutemen for God

Minutemen in the Revolutionary War were armed American civilians who maintained readiness for instant military service. The aged saint minister or layperson must maintain instant readiness to serve God upon being summoned, regardless of prior treatment (being ignored, overlooked, sidestepped, forgotten), as did Daniel.

Just for laughs

Three old ladies were sitting in a diner, chatting about various things. One lady said, "You know, I'm getting really forgetful. This morning I was standing at the top of the stairs, and I couldn't remember whether I had just come up or was about to go down."

The second lady said, "You think that's bad? The other day I was sitting on the edge of my bed, and I couldn't remember whether I was going to bed or had just woken up!"

The third lady smiled smugly. "Well, my memory is just as good as it's always been, knock on wood." She rapped the table. With a startled look on her face, she asked, "Who's there?"[221]

Three boys were in the schoolyard bragging about their fathers. The first boy said, "My Dad scribbles a few words on a piece of paper; he calls it a poem. They give him $50."

The second boy said, "That's nothing. My Dad scribbles a few words on a piece of paper; he calls it a song. They give him $100."

The third boy says, "I got you both beat. My Dad scribbles a few words on a piece of paper, he calls it a sermon, and it takes eight people to collect all the money!"[222]

I know both how to have a little, and I know how to have a lot. In any and all circumstances I have learned the secret of being content. ~ Paul (Philippians 4:12 HCSB)

We do have the choice to be content with where we are in life. I have to admit that I miss the days of driving a car, but I am grateful for those who take me where I need to go. My aches and pains remind me that I'm not as young as I would like to be, but I am thankful I am still here to talk about them. Even at ninety-two my desire is to learn to be content.[223] ~ Billy Graham

I can't help saying to the Lord, "Haven't I had enough years? Wouldn't this be a nice time to take me home?" I realize that it's none of my business when God wants to lift me up there.[224]

~ Elizabeth Elliot

Please don't forget—God has decided to let you live this long. Your old age is not a mistake...nor an oversight...nor an after-thought. Isn't it about time you cooled your tongue and softened your smile with a refreshing drink from the water of God's oasis? You've been thirsty a long, long time.[225] ~ Chuck Swindoll

20

Don't Pine for Death

The great evangelist George Whitefield met with Mr. Tennant and other ministers in New Jersey, during which time he related his difficulties in ministry. He shared that he was weary and worn and was glad that shortly it would be over. Whitefield said he took comfort in knowing soon he would be with the Lord. He then inquired of the others if such was their view. All assented except for Mr. Tennant, who sat next to Whitefield.

Whitefield tapped him on the knee and said, "Well, Brother Tennant, you are the oldest among us; do you not rejoice to think that your time is so near at hand when you will be called Home?" The old man answered that he had no wish about it. When pressed again to answer he said, "No Sir, it is no pleasure to me at all; and if you knew your duty, it would be none to you." The old man continued, "I have nothing to do with death. My business is to live as long as I can and as well as I can and serve my Savior as faithfully as I can until He thinks it's time to call me Home."

Whitefield and the other ministers graciously received the pleasant reproof as of the Lord. It helped Whitefield to continue his work with patience and calm.[226]

Likewise, may the wisdom of Mr. Tennant prove to be just as valuable to you as you battle the difficulties of old age. Leave the matter of death in God's sovereign hand and make the best of what time you have left serving the Lord as faithfully as possible. Remember that what is bad can become good, and even if it doesn't, God will give you coping grace to manage it.

God will give grace to say with Habakkuk: "Even though the fig trees have no blossoms, and there are no grapes on the vines; even though the olive crop fails, and the fields lie empty and barren; even though the flocks die in the fields, and the cattle barns are empty, yet I will rejoice in the LORD! I will be joyful in the God of my salvation! The Sovereign LORD is my strength! He makes me as surefooted as a deer, able to tread upon the heights" (Habakkuk 3:17–19 NLT).

It may bring consolation to know that the Apostle Paul longed to be with the Lord but refused to hurry it along. He says, "To me, living means having Christ. To die means that I would have more of Him. If I keep on living here in this body, it means that I can lead more people to Christ" (Philippians 1:21–22 NLV). Though desirous to be with the Lord immediately, he realized God's purpose for his life had not been finished.

As I write, signs of an early spring are viewed from my office window. And with its arrival there's new life in much of God's creation. Can you imagine a plant, bush or tree saying, "No! I refuse to bring forth new life—I'd rather just die?" The thought is absurd!

Sadly, many in God's garden today want to give up and die instead of bearing new blooms, pedals, leaves and fruit.[227]

Perhaps it's the difficulties, loneliness and sickness of old age that prompt it. But I think it probably has more to do with loss of purpose. It was Paul's purpose that kept him going until it was God's will to take him home. The same is testified to by myriads of aged saints.

Things the elderly can do

Outside of utilizing, if possible, the spiritual gift(s) God bestowed upon you at salvation (see 1 Corinthians 12; Ephesians 4 and Romans 12), engage in other facets of ministry. All, regardless of age or frailty, can encourage a pastor, missionary and other "senior saints." The aged can be a financial helper to a ministerial student, evangelist or missionary. As a young pastor and minister-

Don't Pine for Death

ial student, I was greatly helped and blessed by the weekly five dollars an elderly church member named Emma Todd gave me.

The elderly saint also can edify other believers through studying the Word with them; praying continuously for God's work and workers; sharing God's love through post cards, letters and emails; baking and cooking meals and cakes for the needy; volunteering to work at a hospital, church or nursing facility; doing missionary work, if health allows; serving as a deacon, elder and/or teacher; proclaiming "God's strength to the next generation" (Psalm 71:17–18); recounting God's mighty works to the next generation (Psalm 78:1-8).

Often discovered among the things you like to do are ministry opportunities.

You have heard it said that happiness is a choice. Well so are life and service to God choices. When I was a student at New Orleans Baptist Theological Seminary, a professor told our class something I have never forgotten. He said, "Young men, between the great things for God you cannot do and the little things you are unwilling to do lies the danger that you will do nothing." Age may prevent you from doing "big" things for God, but it certainly cannot and must not keep you back from doing the "little" things.

A soldier strayed from his troop and finally joined the ranks of another army regiment. Immediately he asked an officer, "What can I do?"

"Fall in anywhere," the officer replied, "there's good fighting all along the line." Good advice for the believer with regard to Christian service. Fall in anywhere, for within and without the walls of the church there is plenty of ministry to be done.

Flow through me, Lord, a weak and earthly vessel,
Cleansed by Thy blood and quickened at Thy call.
Flow through me, Lord, all utterly abandoned
To Thy dear service, great or high or small. ~ Anonymous

Aging Honorably and Happily

Just for laughs

A couple had been married for fifty years. "Things have really changed," she said. "You used to sit very close to me."

"Well, I can remedy that," he said, moving next to her on the couch.

"And you used to hold me tight."

"How's that?" he asked as he gave her a hug.

"Do you remember you used to nudge my neck and nibble on my ear lobes?" He jumped to his feet and left the room. "Where are you going?"

"I'll be right back," he said. "I've got to get my teeth!"[228]

One Sunday a pastor told the congregation that the church needed some extra money and asked the people to prayerfully consider giving a little extra in the offering plate. He said that whoever gave the most would be able to pick out three hymns.

After the offering plates were passed, the pastor glanced down and noticed that someone had placed a $1,000 bill in one of them. He was so excited that he immediately shared his joy with his congregation and said he'd like to personally thank the person who placed the money in the plate. A very quiet, elderly, saintly lady all the way in the back shyly raised her hand. The pastor asked her to come to the front. Slowly she made her way to the pastor. He told her how wonderful it was that she gave so much and in thanksgiving asked her to pick out three hymns.

Don't Pine for Death

Her eyes brightened as she looked over the congregation. Then, pointing to the three handsomest men in the building, she said, "I'll take him and him and him."[229]

The greatest legacy one can pass on to one's children and grandchildren is not money or other material things accumulated in one's life, but rather a legacy of character and faith.[230]

~ Billy Graham

No legacy is so rich as honesty. ~ William Shakespeare, *All's Well That Ends Well*

There is nothing more disgraceful than that an old man should have nothing to produce as a proof that he has lived long except his years.[231] ~ Lucius Annaeus Seneca

The measure of a life, after all, is not its duration, but its donation.[232] ~ Peter Marshall

21

A Lasting Legacy

What is a Legacy?

Merriam-Webster Student Dictionary defines *legacy* as "something left to a person by or as if by will." The gift given may be money, houses or lands. It may also be spiritual or godly in nature as in someone's leaving a *legacy* of godly character and faith, which is far more valuable.

A survey among those eighty-five years of age was undertaken in which they were asked to share things they regretted most about their lives. Three things topped the list. Respondents said: 1) I would have spent more time in reflection, in meditation and contemplation. 2) I would have risked more. 3) I would have done more things that would live on after I die.

The third regret cited by the seniors speaks of the absence of having created a lasting spiritual legacy—that which lives on after our death.

Biblical mandate to establish a godly legacy

God instructs us to be intentional about leaving a godly legacy in Deuteronomy 6. "You must commit yourselves wholeheartedly to these commands I am giving you today. Repeat them again and again to your children. Talk about them when you are at home and when you are on the road, when you are going to bed and when you are getting up. Tie them to your hands and wear them on your forehead as reminders. Write them on the doorposts of your house and on your gates" (Deuteronomy 6:6–9 NLT).

The text clearly validates Adrian Rogers' view on legacy building when he said, "Leaving a legacy is a day in, day out, week in, week out, year in, year out way of life."[233]

Aging Honorably and Happily

In Psalm 78 we are again instructed regarding establishing a godly legacy. "We will not hide these truths from our children; we will tell the next generation about the glorious deeds of the Lord, about his power and his mighty wonders" (Psalm 78:4 NLT).

It's dangerous to *hide these truths* of God from our children and grandchildren. Dr. James Dobson cautions, "Today, if we don't intentionally pass a legacy consistent with our beliefs to our children, our culture will pass along its own, often leading to a negative end."[234]

Elijah's legacy to his disciple Elisha

It is obvious from the two texts referenced above that as parents/grandparents, our mandate clearly is to teach our children/grandchildren about the Lord by example and principle. As Elijah passed his mantle on to Elisha, just so we are to pass our faith, convictions, morality, worldview, integrity and biblical view on to them (1 Kings 19:19–21). "What an important investment it is," states Chuck Swindoll, "to pass on to our children a proper scale of values so that they know how to handle the good things of life, knowing that those good things are just a wisp—here today and gone tomorrow. Such an investment also teaches them how to handle it when things aren't easy."[235]

Legacies as footprints in the sand

Godly legacies are like footprints in the sand that are left for others to follow long after our death. Chuck Swindoll said, "Legacies are created. What we do today becomes our legacy tomorrow—either positive or negative."

Jonathan Edwards' legacy

The godly legacy of Jonathan Edwards for his 11 children is revealed by research by American educator and pastor A. E. Winship who traced the descendants of Edwards for almost 150 years after his death.

A Lasting Legacy

Its remarkable findings indicated that Edwards' godly legacy includes one U.S. vice-president, three U.S. senators, three governors, three mayors, thirteen college presidents, thirty judges, sixty-five professors, eighty public office holders, one hundred lawyers and one hundred missionaries.

Most certainly Edwards' investment in building a godly legacy paid off. It always does—but not without disciplined effort. Solomon said, "The good people who live honest lives will be a blessing to their children" (Proverbs 20:7 NCV). Edwards was; you may be too.

> Though a financial legacy may have its value, remember that in the long haul it's not what we give others but what we instill in others that counts the most for time and eternity.

A lasting legacy

Though a financial or materialistic legacy may have its value, remember that in the long haul it's not *what we give others but what we instill in others* that counts the most for time and eternity.

Dr. James Dobson cautions, "Today, if we don't intentionally pass a legacy consistent with our beliefs to our children, our culture will pass along its own, often leading to a negative end."[236]

Will the legacy you leave be lasting? Will it be imperishable and eternal? Or will it be tangible (money or possessions) and temporal?

Work tirelessly to carve into the hearts of those whom you love godly affirmations, convictions and values by example and precept. Remember, a godly legacy won't just happen. It must be tediously and prayerfully built.

Aging Honorably and Happily

Just for Laughs

Walking up to a department store's fabric counter, a pretty girl asked, "I want to buy this material for a new dress. How much does it cost?"

"Only one kiss per yard," replied the smirking male clerk.

"That's fine," replied the girl. "I'll take ten yards."

With expectation and anticipation written all over his face, the clerk hurriedly measured out and wrapped the cloth, then held it out teasingly. The girl snapped up the package and pointed to a little old man standing beside her. "Grandpa will pay the bill," she smiled.[237]

Q. Why did the duck go to jail?

A: Because he got caught selling quack.

Many characteristics we associate with older age—like the inability to walk long distances, climb stairs, or carry groceries—are largely due to a lack of physical activity.[238]

~ Dr. John Montgomery

Having someone prod you to get out and exercise might not make you feel loved in the short run—in fact, it may be quite irritating. But it can be very effective in getting people to change their behaviors in positive ways.[239]

~ Joan Tucker, Behavioral Scientist

If someone's a smoker, they gotta stop. Even quitting in your seventies improves survival. If patients want to do one thing for their health, it would be to stop smoking.[240]

~ Stuart Connolly, M.D.

For "physical exercise has some value, but godliness is valueble in every way. It holds promise for the present life and for the life to come." ~ 1 Timothy 4:8 NET

22

Get Up and Move: The Benefit of Exercise

Inactivity contributes to sickness and injury among the aging; therefore, exercise has its value, as Paul stipulates (I Timothy 4:8). Studies reveal that there are many health benefits to be derived from staying physically active as older adults. Yet sixty percent of people over the age of sixty-four are considered sedentary according to a report by the AARP. Prior to the knowledge of the health benefits of exercise as known today, Edward Stanley (1826–1893) made a remarkable statement: "Those who think they have no time for bodily exercise will sooner or later have to find time for illness."[241]

As a runner for some thirty-five years (50,000 miles and counting), I assuredly can attest to the value of exercise. Nothing is wasted in whatever form of exercise you undertake or for whatever duration. Something is always better than nothing in regard to exercise.

The Centers for Disease Control reports that the elderly have more to gain through exercise than those younger because they are at higher risk for the health issues that exercise can prevent.[242]

Even moderate exercise can benefit seniors.

Increases longevity

Ezra Fishman, part of Penn's Population Studies Center, and the other researchers looked at data from approximately 3,000 people aged 50 to 79 who participated in the National Health and Nutrition Examination Survey conducted by the Centers for Disease Control and Prevention.

The study revealed that the least active were five times more likely to die during that period than the most active. "When we compare people who exercise the same amount, those who sit less and move around more tend to live longer," said Fishman, the lead author on the paper. He further added, "The folks who were walking around, washing the dishes, sweeping the floor tended to live longer than the people who were sitting at a desk."[243]

Enhances cardiovascular health

Exercise benefits the cardiovascular system immensely. The heart, like all muscles, strengthens as a result of exercise enabling it to pump more blood through the body with every beat and keep working at a maximum level, if necessary, with less effort or strain.

Maintaining a healthy cardiovascular system through exercise assists in the prevention of a heart attack and stroke. The American College of Cardiology/American Heart Association recommends at least thirty minutes of moderate (at 50–70% of maximum predicted heart rate) exercise on most days to reduce the risk of cardiovascular problems.

According to *Health Times* published by the *New York Times,* some studies suggest it's not the duration of a single exercise that counts but the weekly cumulative amount of energy expended that gives the greatest heart protection.[244]

Increases mental capacity

Exercise supplies oxygen to the brain which helps with increased mental capacity. Tucker Sutherland, editor of the *Senior Journal* states, "Exercise equals better mental performance as people age."[245] Additionally, if exercise is begun when young and continued regularly, it is beneficial in preventing dementia and Alzheimer's disease.[246]

Increases rapid healing

It's common knowledge that the older one becomes the longer it takes for wounds and injuries to heal. Regular exercise can speed up the healing in seniors by as much as twenty-five percent.[247]

Improves musculoskeletal health

Exercise may significantly improve musculoskeletal and overall health and minimize or delay the effects of aging.[248]

Helps chronic conditions

In some cases, regular exercise is an effective treatment for people with arthritis, heart disease, diabetes or high blood pressure.[249]

Increases balance

Exercise prevents falls which lead to broken hips and other debilitating injuries which force dependency upon others. The Mayo Clinic states, "Nearly any activity that keeps you on your feet and moving, such as walking, can help you maintain good balance. But specific exercises designed to enhance your balance are beneficial to include in your daily routine and can help to improve your stability."[250]

Increases flexibility

As we grow older our muscles become shorter and lose their elasticity causing decreases in range of motion. Stretching exercises help to increase motion control or flexibility. Stretching exercises also help with the aches and pains from muscle and joint stiffness.

"Flexibility is the third pillar of fitness, next to cardiovascular conditioning and strength training," says David Geier, the director of sports medicine at the Medical University of South Carolina in Charleston and a spokesperson for the American Orthopedic Society for Sports Medicine.[251]

Geier states that flexibility may prevent injury and even contribute to staving off arthritis and more serious illnesses.[252]

Aging Honorably and Happily

Stretching exercises may improve your circulation which increases blood flow to the muscles. And good circulation helps ward off many illnesses from diabetes to kidney disease. A 2009 study in the *American Journal of Physiology* revealed that greater flexibility is linked to a lower risk of cardiovascular disease.[253]

Improves quality of life

A Harvard Medical School report states, "In addition to making your heart and muscles stronger and fending off a host of diseases, it [exercise] can also improve your mental and emotional functioning and even bolster your productivity and close relationships."[254] It helps you maintain independence longer, thwarts depression and enhances mobility.

Boosts mood

Exercise is a huge stress reliever. Endorphins produced through exercise can actually help reduce feelings of sadness, depression, or anxiety.[255]

Weight reduction

According to physicians being mildly overweight bears little harm, but being too much overweight actually is hazardous for an aging body. Sarah Varney states, "Obesity increases inflammation, exacerbates bone and muscle loss and significantly raises the risk of heart disease, stroke and diabetes."[256] "Maintaining a healthy weight is one of the best things you can do for your heart" says Richard Wright, M.D.[257]

Enhances sleep

Research is showing that exercise impacts the overall quality of sleep. It may well serve as a "nonpharmaceutical alternative to improve sleep," said Brad Cardinal, a professor of exercise science at Oregon State University and one of the study's authors.[258]

Get Up and Move: The Benefit of Exercise

Consistency not intensity is the key

"When it comes to exercise for seniors, consistency is more important than intensity," explains Dr. John Montgomery. "Moderate exercise, such as walking five or more days a week, can lead to substantial health benefits. Even brief amounts of physical activity, say ten minutes at a time, can be beneficial."[259]

For many years I had a poster hung in my study that showed a runner on a stretch of road that appeared to go for miles. Beneath the picture was a caption that read: "The race doesn't belong to the swift or the quick but to those who keep running." And I add "or keep walking."

Oldest also benefit from exercise

According to the National Institute of Aging, exercise is beneficial not just for *young* older folk but for those who are 80, 90 or older.

Stay hydrated

"Every day you lose water through your breath, perspiration, urine and bowel movements. For your body to function properly, you must replenish its water supply by consuming beverages and foods that contain water."[260] With regard to how much water you should drink, the Mayo Clinic states that water needs vary based on numerous factors, including health, activity and geographical location.

"The Institute of Medicine determined that an adequate intake (AI) for men is roughly about 13 cups (3 liters) of total beverages a day. The AI for women is about 9 cups (2.2 liters) of total beverages a day."[261] All fluids, not just water, count toward the daily total.[262] Keep in mind certain health conditions will impact water consumption limits, so if you are sick, check with your doctor prior to increasing water intake.

Aging Honorably and Happily

Staying adequately hydrated assists in lowering blood pressure naturally and keeps the organs and digestive tract running efficiently.

Six myths about the elderly and exercise

Exercise Myth: Decline in old age is inevitable; therefore, exercise is pointless.

Your being elderly doesn't mean you are decrepit. There are people that are in their eighties and nineties running marathons.[263]

Exercise Myth: It's not safe for the elderly to exercise; they may fall, dislocating their hip.

Studies reveal that exercise actually may reduce your chance of a fall.[264]

Exercise Myth: People with medical conditions shouldn't exercise.

On the contrary, exercise can help with arthritis, heart disease, and diabetes. "Exercise is almost like a silver bullet for lots of health problems."[265]

Exercise Myth: A heart attack might result.

Heart attacks do occur during exercise, but the many benefits of exercise overshadow its small risk.[266]

Exercise Myth: If you haven't exercised all your life, it's too late to begin when you're old.

Research proves this is just not true. People in their nineties have benefited from exercise.[267]

Exercise Myth: Running is better exercise than walking.

Running is more effective for weight loss than walking is, but the loss of weight is only one of many reasons why we need to exercise. In its journal *Arteriosclerosis, Thrombosis and Vascular*

Get Up and Move: The Benefit of Exercise

Biology, the American Heart Association reported that moderately paced walking is just as effective as running in reducing blood pressure, cholesterol levels, and the risk for heart disease and diabetes.[268] The principal author of the study, Dr. Paul T. Williams, said "The more the runners ran and the more the walkers walked, the better off they were in health benefits. If the amount of energy expended was the same between the two groups, then the health benefits were comparable."[269]

Secrets of aging well (physical aspect)

A Harvard study states that focus upon the following factors are predictive as to how successful you will move through middle age and into your eighties.

Avoiding cigarettes
Good adjustment or coping skills ("making lemonade out of lemons")
Keeping a healthy weight
Exercising regularly
Maintaining strong social relationships (including a stable marriage)
Pursuing education[270]

Don't overdo it

Remember, if you cannot carry on a conversation while exercising, most likely you are overdoing it.

Physician consultation

Prior to embarking upon an exercise routine, it is advisable to consult with your doctor for approval, guidance and, if necessary, referral to a gerontologist.

Aging Honorably and Happily

Just for laughs

Thought I'd let my doctor check me
'Cause I didn't feel quite right;
All those aches and pains annoyed me,
And I couldn't get to sleep at night.

He could find no real disorder,
But he couldn't let me rest;
What with Medicare and Blue Cross
It wouldn't hurt to do some tests.

To the hospital he sent me,
Though I didn't feel that bad;
He arranged for them to give me
Every test that could be had.

I was fluoroscoped and cystoscoped,
My aging frame displayed,
Stripped upon an ice-cold table
While my gizzards were X-rayed.

I was checked for worms and parasites,
For fungus and the crud
While they pierced me with long needles,
Taking samples of my blood.

Doctors came to check me over,
Prodded and pushed and poked around;
And to make sure that I was living,
They wired me up for sound.

Get Up and Move: The Benefit of Exercise

They have finally concluded
(Their results have filled a page)
What I have will someday kill me;
My affliction is...old age. ~ Unknown

I got another letter from this lawyer today. It said, "Final Notice." Good that he will not bother me anymore. [271]

Whatever poet, orator, or sage may say of it, old age is still old age.[272] ~ Henry Wadsworth Longfellow

The time of old age, with all its infirmities, seems to me to be a time of peculiar blessedness and privilege to the Christian. To the worldly sinner, whose zest for pleasure has been removed by the debility of his powers and the decay of his strength, old age must be a season of tedium and pain.[273] ~ C. H. Spurgeon

I am much clearer now. I say that as an older person—not just as an adult, but as an older person—things are much clearer. I was just telling my daughter, "I think I'm happier now than I've ever been in my life."[274] ~ Cecile, age 93

We are not yet what we shall be, but we are growing toward it. The process is not yet finished, but it is going on. This is not the end, but it is the road. All does not yet gleam in glory, but all is being purified.[275] ~ Martin Luther

23

Old Age: Adages and Reflections from Great Saints

Old age ˌōld ˈāj/—the state of being old

"The glory of young men is their strength: and the beauty of old men is the gray head" (Proverbs 20:29). Solomon, in contrasting various ages in life, states that each has a purpose, function and duty that must not be despised or deserted. All are needful and useful in the church and to one another. Old age is a gift to be enjoyed, not a curse to be endured; a blessing, not a burden.

To help you determine if you are growing old, examine the following description of what it might look like.

You know you're growing old when

The gleam in your eyes is from the sun hitting your glasses.
You feel like the night before, and you haven't been anywhere.
Your little black book contains only names ending in "M.D."
You get winded playing chess.
Your children look middle-aged.
You finally reach the top of the ladder, only to find it leaning against the wrong wall.
You join a health club and don't go.
You decide to procrastinate, but then you never get around to it.
Your mind makes contracts your body can't meet.
You know all the answers, but nobody asks you the questions.
You look forward to a dull evening.
You walk with your head held high, trying to get used to your trifocals.
Your favorite part of the newspaper is "25 Years Ago Today."
You sit in a rocking chair and can't get it going.
Your knees buckle, and your belt won't.
You stop looking forward to your next birthday.

Aging Honorably and Happily

Dialing long distance wears you out.

You just can't stand people who are intolerant.

The best part of the day is over when your alarm clock goes off.

You burn the midnight oil after 9:00 p.m.

Your back goes out more than you do.

A fortune teller offers to read your face.

The little gray-haired lady you help across the street is your wife.

You sink your teeth into a steak and they stay there. ~ Unknown

Reflections

Charles Haddon Spurgeon on growing old

"His comforts you will never be able to exhaust in all your life, but you will find that the bottle of your joys will be as full when you have been drinking seventy years as it was when you first began."[276]

John Piper on growing old

"Getting old to the glory of God means getting old in a way that makes God look glorious. It means living and dying in a way that shows God to be the all-satisfying Treasure that He is. So it would include, for example, not living in ways that makes this world look like your treasure."[277]

Henry Wilson on growing old

"For twenty-one years it has been not only a living reality to me, but a reality growing deeper and richer, until now at the age of seventy years, I am in every sense a younger, fresher man than I was at thirty. At this present time I am in the strength of God doing full twice as much work, mental and physical, as I have ever done in the best days of the past, and this observe, with less than half the effort then necessary. My life, physical, mental and spiritual, is like an artesian well—always full, overflowing. To speak, teach, travel by night and day in all weather and through all the sudden and violent changes of our variable climate is no more effort to me than it is for the mill-wheel to turn when the stream is full or for the pipe to let the water run through." [278]

John Wesley on growing old

On his eighty-fifth birthday (June 28, 1788), John Wesley wrote in his journal (paraphrased):

"It is true that I am not as agile or able to run or walk as fast as when younger. Also, there is some decay in my memory in regard to names and things lately passed, but not at all with what I read or heard twenty, forty, or sixty years ago. I do not encounter any weariness in traveling or preaching, or any decay in the writing of sermons. To what cause can I attribute this? First, to the power of God fitting me to the work to which I am called; and next, to the prayers of His children. Then may not I also impute it to these inferior means:

1. My constant exercise and change of air
2. My never having lost a night's sleep, sick or well, on land or at sea
3. My having slept at command, whether day or night
4. My having risen constantly at 4:00 a.m. for about sixty years.
5. My constant preaching at 5:00 a.m. for above fifty years.
6. My having so little pain, sorrow, or anxious care in life."[279]

Henry Durbanville on growing old

"I feel so sorry for folks who don't like to grow old. I revel in my years. They enrich me. I would not exchange the abiding rest of soul, the measure of wisdom I have gained from the sweet and bitter and perplexing experiences of life, nor the confirmed faith I now have in the love of God, for all the bright and uncertain hopes and tumultuous joys of youth. Indeed, I would not! These are the best years of my life. The way grows brighter; the birds sing sweeter; the winds blow softer; the sun shines more radiantly than ever before. I suppose 'my outward man' is perishing, but 'my inward man' is being joyously renewed day by day."[280]

Robertson McQuilkin on growing old

"God planned the strength and beauty of youth to be physical. But the strength and beauty of age is spiritual. We gradually lose the strength and beauty that is temporary so we'll be sure to concentrate on the strength and beauty that is forever."[281]

Lyman Beecher on growing old

Lyman Beecher (October 12, 1775–January 10, 1863) was a minister. A man said to him in his old age, "Doctor, you have lived a long time and have seen and have known many things; what do you consider the main thing?"

The old veteran replied, "It is not theology; it is not controversy; it is the saving of souls."[282]

Paul Tournier on growing old

"Your manner of life now is already determining your life in those years of old age and retirement, without your realizing it even, and perhaps without your giving enough thought to it. One must therefore prepare oneself for retirement."[283]

Dr. Baldwin on growing old

Dr. Baldwin, who was pastor of a church for forty-one years, says, "With another, I testify that at thirty, after examining as best I could the philosophies and religions of the world, I said, 'Nothing is better than the Gospel of Christ.' At forty, when burdens began to press heavily and years seemed to hasten, I said, 'Nothing is as good as the Gospel.'

Old Age: Adages and Reflections from Great Saints

"At fifty, when there were empty chairs in the home and the mound builders had done me service, I said, 'There is nothing to be compared with the Gospel.' At sixty, when my second sight saw through the delusions and vanities of earthly things, I said, 'There is nothing but the Gospel.' At seventy, amid many limitations and deprivations, I sing

> Should all the forms that men devise
> > Attack my faith with treacherous art,
> I'd call them vanities and lies
> > And bind the Gospel to my heart."[284]

Chuck Swindoll on growing old

"As you look into the mirror, you're forced to admit that the fingers of age have begun to scratch their marks upon your house of clay...and it's hard to believe your twilight years could be of any worth. How wrong! How terribly wrong! How destructive such thoughts can be! How quickly such thinking can sentence you to the prison cell of self-pity surrounded by the four bleak walls of doubt, depression, uselessness, and grief.

"God's patriarchs have always been among His choicest possessions. Abraham was far more effective once he grew old and mellow. Moses wasn't used with any measure of success until he turned eighty. Caleb was eighty-five when he began to enjoy God's best goals. Samuel was old, old when the God of Israel led him to establish the 'school of the prophets,' an institution that had a lasting influence for spirituality and godliness in the centuries to come. And who could deny the way God used Paul during his last days on his knees, writing words of encouragement in letters we cherish today!"[285]

Max Lucado on growing old

Aging Honorably and Happily

"Growing old can be dangerous. The trail is treacherous, and the pitfalls are many. One is wise to be prepared. You know it's coming. It's not like God kept the process a secret. It's not like you are blazing a trail as you grow older. It's not as if no one has ever done it before. Look around you. You have ample opportunity to prepare and ample case studies to consider. If growing old catches you by surprise, don't blame God. He gave you plenty of warning. He also gave you plenty of advice."[286]

Billy Graham on growing old

First, accept it as part of God's plan for your life and thank Him every day for the gift of that day. We've come to look on old age as something to be dreaded—and it's true that it isn't easy. I can't honestly say that I like being old—not being able to do most of the things I used to do, for example, and being more dependent on others and facing physical challenges that I know will only get worse. Old age can be a lonely time also—children scattered, spouse and friends gone.

But God has a reason for keeping us here (even if we don't always understand it), and we need to recover the Bible's understanding of life and longevity as gifts from God—and therefore as something good. Several times the Bible mentions people who died 'at a good old age'—an *interesting* phrase (emphasis added). So part of my advice is to learn to be content, and that only comes as we accept each day as a gift from God and commit it into his hands. Paul's words are true at every stage of life but especially as we grow older: "Godliness with contentment is great gain" (1 Timothy 6:6)."[287]

John MacArthur on growing old

"And just because you're growing old, life doesn't have to be bleak. I mean it's...it's certainly for a Christian to be rewarded as a crowning time of life with a level of spiritual maturity you can't have in your youth. All those who know Christ, all those who have

Old Age: Adages and Reflections from Great Saints

walked with Him for any length of time should look forward to old age because it takes us nearer to Heaven, doesn't it? It puts us in a situation where we have accumulated spiritual experience, which makes us truly rich. It enables us to be the leaders and the mentors and the models and the examples for the young. It allows us to filter out life and keep what we think is really valuable. Should be a good time."[288]

G. Campbell Morgan on growing old

"It is a great thing to find that, even though vigor decreases, the light on the road abides; and though early shadows may be lengthening, one does not feel one is going downhill, but rather up."[289]

W. Somerset Maugham on growing old

"The complete life, the perfect pattern, includes old age as well as youth and maturity. The beauty of the morning and the radiance of noon are good, but it would be a very silly person who drew the curtains and turned on the light in order to shut out the tranquility of the evening. Old age has its pleasures, which, though different, are not less than the pleasures of youth."[290]

Adages

"The spiritual eyesight improves as the physical eyesight declines." ~ Plato

"You are never too old to set a new goal or dream a new dream."[291] ~ Les Brown

"The seven ages of man: spills, drills, thrills, bills, ills, pills, wills."[292] ~ Richard Needham

"Someday you will be old enough to start reading fairy tales again."[293] ~ C. S. Lewis

Aging Honorably and Happily

"Those who love deeply never grow old; they may die of old age, but they die young." ~ Benjamin Franklin.

"The greatest tribute to the dead is not grief but gratitude."[294] ~ Thornton Wilder

"I'm not eighty. I am four times twenty." ~ Daniel Auber

"For the first half of your life, people tell you what you should do; for the second half, they tell you what you should have done."
~ Richard Needham

"The first half of life consists of the capacity to enjoy without the chance; the last half consists of the chance without the capacity."[295] ~ Mark Twain

"About the time your face clears up, your mind gets fuzzy."[296]
~ James Dobson

"If you would keep young: be cheerful, keep working, and love one another."[297] ~ Fanny J. Crosby

"Every man desires to live long, but no man wishes to be old."
~ Jonathan Swift

"You are as young as your faith, as old as your doubt; as young as your self-confidence, as old as your fear; as young as your hope, as old as your despair." ~ Douglas MacArthur

"The more the marble wears, the better the image grows."
~ Michelangelo

"The years teach much which the days never knew."[298]
~ Ralph Waldo Emerson

Old Age: Adages and Reflections from Great Saints

"None are so old as those who have outlived enthusiasm."
~ Henry David Thoreau

"A man is not old until regrets take the place of dreams."
~ Unknown

"Age is not a particularly interesting subject. Anyone can get old. All you have to do is live long enough." ~ Groucho Marx

"Don't worry about avoiding temptation—as you grow older, it starts avoiding you." ~ Author Unknown

"Old age is ready to undertake tasks that youth shirked because they would take too long."[299] ~ W. Somerset Maugham

"A man in old age is like a sword in a shop window. Men that look upon the perfect blade do not imagine the process by which it was completed."[300] ~ Henry Ward Beecher

"What's a man's age? He must hurry more, that's all;
Cram in a day what his youth took a year to hold."[301]
~ Robert Browning

"Old age is like everything else. To make a success of it, you've got to start young."[302] ~ President Theodore Roosevelt

"Birthdays are good for you. The more you have the longer you live." ~ Unknown

"When grace is joined with wrinkles, it is adorable. There is an unspeakable dawn in happy old age." ~ Victor Hugo

"Count your life by smiles, not tears.
Count your age by friends, not years." ~ Unknown

Aging Honorably and Happily

"The solitude in which we are left by the death of our friends is one of the great evils of protracted life. When I look back to the days of my youth, it is like looking over a field of battle. All, all dead! and ourselves left alone midst a new generation whom we know not and who know not us."[303] ~ President Thomas Jefferson

"We don't stop playing because we grow old; we grow old because we stop playing." ~ George Bernard Shaw

"Age and youth look upon life from the opposite ends of the telescope; it is exceedingly long—it is exceedingly short."[304]
~ Henry Ward Beecher

"Preparation for old age should begin no later than one's teens. A life which is empty of purpose until 65 will not suddenly become filled on retirement."[305] ~ D. L. Moody

"The heart never grows better by age; I fear rather worse, always harder. A young liar will be an old one, and a young knave [a dishonest or unscrupulous man] will only be a greater knave as he grows older."[306] ~ Lord Chesterfield

"The greatest tragedy of old age is the tendency for the old to feel unneeded, unwanted, and of no use to anyone; the secret of happiness in the declining years is to remain interested in life, as active as possible, useful to others, busy, and forward looking."[307]
~ Eleanor Roosevelt

"Don't resent growing old. Many are denied the privilege." ~ Unknown

"The wiser mind mourns less for what age takes away than what it leaves behind."[308] ~ William Wordsworth

Old Age: Adages and Reflections from Great Saints

Dora Johnson wrote,

You tell me I am getting old;
I tell you that's not so.
The "house" I live in is worn out—
And that, of course, I know.

It's been in use a long, long while;
It's weathered many a gale.
I'm really not surprised you think
It's getting somewhat frail.

The color's changing on the roof;
The windows getting dim,
The walls a bit transparent
And looking rather thin.

The foundation's not so steady
As once it used to be;
My "house" is getting shaky,
But my "house" isn't me!

My few short years can't make me old—
I feel I'm in my youth;
Eternity lies just ahead,
A life of joy and truth.

I'm going to live forever there;
Life will go on—it's grand!
You tell me I am getting old?
You just don't understand!

The dweller in my little "house"
Is young and bright and gay—
Just starting on a life to last
Throughout eternal day.

Aging Honorably and Happily

You only see the outside,
Which is all that most folks see.
You tell me I am getting old?
You've mixed my "house" with me!

Just for laughs

The comedian Sam Levenson said, "If you die in an elevator, be sure to push the up button."

Our pastor called the other day and told my wife, Helen, that at her age she should start thinking about the hereafter. "Oh, I do, I do," Helen told him. "No matter where I am, I ask myself, 'What am I here after?'" ~ Source Unknown

At evening time it shall be light. ~ Zechariah 14:7

Autumn is really the best of the seasons; and I'm not sure that old age isn't the best part of life.[309] ~ C. S. Lewis

How strange this fear of death is! We are never frightened at a sunset.[310] ~ George MacDonald

I can only say that I am more and more convinced as I grow older that to keep our eyes steadily fixed on the second coming of Christ is one great secret of Christian peace.[311] ~ J. C. Ryle

Remember that some of the brightest drops in the chalice of life may still remain for us in old age. The last draught which a kind Providence gives us to drink, though near the bottom of the cup, may, as is said of the draught of the Roman of old, have at the very bottom, instead of dregs, most costly pearls.[312] ~ W. A. Newman

24

At Evening Time It Shall Be Light

I recall reading as a young man a devotional by the famed London pastor C. H. Spurgeon upon the text: "At evening time it shall be light." It stuck to my mind as if it were glue. Later I discovered a sermon by him upon the same topic, one which provides great hope and comfort to the child of God in the twilight years. In the sermon Spurgeon states, "Dread not thy days of weariness; dread not thine hours of decay, O soldier of the cross. New lights shall burn when the old lights are quenched; new candles shall be lit when the lamps of life are dim. Fear not! The night of thy decay may be coming on, but "at evening time it shall be light." At evening time the Christian has many lights that he never had before, lit by the Holy Spirit and shining by His light."[313] Light is the synonym for joy, being upbeat, and knowledge.

> So the darkness shall be the light, and the stillness the dancing. ~ T. S. Eliot

Spurgeon cites several of these *lights* that will shine at the evening of life for the aged believer. There is the *light of bright experience* for looking back upon life, for he can say, "Hitherto, by thy help I have come." There is the *light of the Bible* whose every promise was proved to be true and trustworthy. And there is the *light of remembrance* regarding rewarding service rendered and lives impacted (some of which were led to Christ).[314]

To Spurgeon's list I add two additional lights. The *light of blessed assurance of salvation*, the confident knowledge in knowing Heaven awaits beyond the realms of this world. To know with Paul that "to be absent from the body is to be present with the Lord" shines bountiful light upon the soul in what otherwise would be a dreaded, gloomy, despairing and hopeless time.

Aging Honorably and Happily

And the other is the *light of divine hope and encouragement*. Oswald Chambers explains, "There is nothing, naturally speaking, that makes us lose heart quicker than decay—the decay of bodily beauty, of natural life, of friendship, of associations. All these things make a man lose heart, but Paul says when we are trusting in Jesus Christ these things do not find us discouraged. Light comes through them."[315]

"At evening time it shall be light" is a glorious promise to those who claim Jesus Christ as their Lord and Savior. But to those who know Him not, the "evening" of life will not be one of "light" but of pain, panic and fear.

In 1915, Fanny Crosby wrote her final hymn, "At Evening Time It Shall be Light." Being in her ninety-fifth year at the time of its writing, the hymn doubtlessly is based upon her experience.

> At evening time it shall be light,
> When fades the day of toil away;
> No shadows deep, no weary night,
> At evening time it shall be light.
> At evening time it shall be light;
> Immortal love from realms above
> Is breathing now the promise bright:
> At evening time it shall be bright.
>
> At evening time it shall be light;
> We'll gather flowers from rural bowers.
> Oh, sacred hope of glory bright,
> At evening time it shall be bright.
> At evening time it shall be light;
> Sweet evening time of joy divine
> That makes the Christians life so bright,
> At evening time it shall be light.

At Evening Time It Shall Be Light

At evening time it shall be light;
No cares shall harm, no fears alarm.
If one in Christ, our souls unite;
At evening time it shall be light.
At evening time it shall be light;
The heart will glow; no tears will flow.
It cannot lose its promise bright:
At evening time it shall be light.

Yes, at "evening time it shall be light," so thrust aside the wardrobe of doubt, fear, dread and panic, and put on the garment of praise, contentment, peace, hope and joy. As T. S. Elliot said, "So the darkness shall be the light, and the stillness the dancing."[316]

Just for laughs

A young man observed an elderly couple at a restaurant about to eat lunch. They had only ordered one meal and had requested an extra drink cup. The young man noticed the old man cutting the hamburger precisely in half and then dividing the French fries exactly in half. Next the man was observed pouring half of the soft drink into the extra cup which sat in front of his wife. The old man began to eat while his wife sat with hands folded in her lap watching.

The young man politely asked the couple if they would permit him to purchase another meal so they wouldn't have to split one between them. The old gentleman said, "Oh, no. We've been married fifty years, and everything has always been and will always be shared 50/50."

The young man then asked of the man's wife if she was going to eat. She replied, "Not yet. It's his turn with the teeth."

Aging Honorably and Happily

Why did the physics teacher break up with the biology teacher? There was no chemistry.

The secret of staying young is to live honestly, eat slowly and lie about your age. ~ Lucille Ball

I had to wait 110 years to become famous. I wanted to enjoy it as long as possible. ~ French supercentenarian Jeanne Louise Calment who died at age 122 (1875–1997)

I have reached an age when, if someone tells me to wear socks, I don't have to. ~ Albert Einstein (1879–1955)

By the time you're eighty years old, you've learned everything. You only have to remember it. ~ George Burns (1896–1996)

25

Fifty-Five Hints to Aging Well from Old-Timers

From those who are older, insights may be learned as to how to age well.

1. Replace the friends who die with younger friends.

2. Drink daily two to three ounces of olive oil (pure, unadulterated) at bedtime.

3. Stay busy (active) as much as possible.

4. Stop worrying. Don't sweat the small stuff.

5. Travel more. Develop a bucket list of places to visit and begin whittling it down.

6. Happiness is a choice. Don't allow circumstances to hinder.

7. Avoid money scams. Never give your Social Security number, credit card account numbers, or bank account numbers to someone on the phone or via email. It is wise to routinely check credit card and checking account statements for possible fraudulent activity.

8. Medicine reminders. Pill boxes are available to store daily dosages for a week at a time. Set up a call alert from a family member or friend to remind you to take medicine if necessary.

9. Eat more fruits and vegetables every day. Katherine Tallmadge, a registered dietitian in Washington, D.C., states, "It's one of the simplest things people can do to transform their health and their lives. We know now that people who eat at least five cups [of fruits and vegetables] a day have lower blood pressure, lower cardiovascular disease, lower rates of cancer; they have a better immune response; usually they're leaner and have lower rates of diabetes and obesity."[317]

10. Change what you can; accept what you cannot.

11. Laugh a lot. Laughter is some of the best medicine you can take for mental, physical and social well-being. A Norway study reveals that people with a strong sense of humor outlive

those who don't laugh as much.[318] My laughter therapy includes watching episodes of Andy Griffith and Hogan Heroes.

12. The way you start the day really matters. An eighty-eight-year-old man said that he greets each day with laughing in the mirror—to start his day in joy.[319]

13. Implement practices that will help you age well—things like caring for the teeth and ears; eating healthy; exercising regularly.[320]

14. Don't view your age as a "handicap."[321]

15. Make sure you have friends twenty years older and twenty years younger all the time (from an eighty-eight-year-old man and a ninety-six-year-old woman).[322]

16. Keep setting new goals; expand your comfort zone.[323]

17. It's never too late to learn.

18. Stay positive.

19. Happiness is not found. It is created.

20. Don't take yourself too seriously.

21. Deflate the ego. You have nothing to prove, no image to maintain and no one to impress.

22. We are not these bodies; they simply are the houses we live in for a little while.

23. "I start to feel very low when I visit old memories, especially the sad ones." Frieda went on to state that she feels the best when she leaves the past alone and is content to accept what happens.[324]

24. "Don't look at the calendar. Just keep celebrating every day."[325] (centenarian)

25. "Don't be a cheapskate."[326] (centenarian)

26. "My inspiration is Robert Browning's poem 'Abt Vogler.' My father used to read it to me. It encourages us to make big art, not small scribbles. It says to try to draw a circle so huge that there is no way we can finish it while we are alive. All we see is an arch; the rest is beyond our vision, but it is there in the distance."[327] (centenarian)

Fifty-Five Hints to Aging Well from Old-Timers

27. "Take naps every day."[328] (centenarian)

28. "I never drank, smoked or fooled with the weeds—you know, that stuff. And I don't let anything upset me, especially traffic."[329] (centenarian)

29. "Do what you have to do. Don't analyze it; just do it."[330] (centenarian)

30. "Find a cause and knock yourself out for it. It will enhance your brainpower and interest in life, and it will keep you alive longer."[331] (centenarian)

31. "To stay healthy always, take the stairs and carry your own stuff."[332] (centenarian)

32. Eat four strips of bacon daily.[333] (centenarian) That's my kind of person!

33. "For breakfast I drink coffee, a glass of milk, and some orange juice with a tablespoon of olive oil in it. Olive oil is great for the arteries."[334] (centenarian)

34. Don't focus on the accumulation of stuff. My father, prior to his death, used to tell us at Christmas not to give him anything he couldn't eat or spend.

35. Be flexible. Learn to adapt to what comes your way.

36. A major regret of old people facing death was that they failed to give cherished friendships the time and effort deserved and allowed them to slip away.[335]

37. Tell people how you truly feel about them. Tomorrow may be too late.

38. Spend more time with the people you love and who love you.

39. Purchase a Fitbit or similar device to monitor and motivate daily activity.

40. Maintain intimate fellowship with the Lord via prayer, Bible study, church worship and ministry service.

41. Memorize Scripture. As one ages, vision may suffer, so store up the Word of God in your heart while vision is good.

42. Take a multivitamin daily (eighty-three-year-old).

43. Each morning before you get out of bed, stretch your entire body for a few seconds. I have found this to be a good practice.

44. Accept and adjust to the seasons of life. Roman orator and statesman Cicero, while in his early sixties, said "Attempting to cling to youth after the appropriate time is useless. If you fight nature, you will lose."[336]

45. Help others. Splash out God's love on them. I shared with my aged saintly mother that I did not see how she could do all that she did in a day. She literally would go nonstop from morning to night many days, all the while battling personal illness. Her busyness and ministry to others kept her "alive" physically, mentally and socially until she was hospitalized and died. Mom refused to give up on life as long as she had life.

46. Don't alienate others. A world of one is a lonely place.

47. "He who is of a calm and happy nature will hardly feel the pressure of age, but to him who is of an opposite disposition, youth and age are equally a burden." Plato (427–346 B.C.)

48. "The years between the ages of 50 and 70 are the hardest. You are always being asked to do more, and you are not yet decrepit enough to turn them down." T. S. Eliot

49. Now deceased missionary Bertha Smith, who almost made it to age one hundred, believed it was essential to drink only water with meals.

50. "There is no time for anything inessential. I must focus on myself, my work and my friends. I shall no longer look at 'News Hour' every night."[337]

51. "[Don't] waste time living in the past and mourning over the failures of yesterday or the long ago."[338]

52. "Arise joyfully," regardless of what you are to face during the day."[339]

Fifty-Five Hints to Aging Well from Old-Timers

53. "Victory is to be attained through the joyful acceptance of annoying trials and petty vexations as part of God's discipline (James 1:2–7)."

54. Know what you are signing. Be attentive to words or clauses like "waiver," "statutes of limitations," "confessions of judgment," "waiver of exemption," and "homestead right." Don't sign contracts/legal papers with blanks in them. If the salesman says, "This is the form everyone signs," don't believe him. Read it first.

55. Shred documents/credit card statements, etc., that contain personal information which a thief could take from the trash bin.

Just for laughs

You know you're old when you ask yourself as you tie your shoes, *Is there anything else I need to do while I'm down here?*

"I'll tell ya how to stay young. Hang around with older people."[340] ~ Bob Hope

"Retirement at sixty-five is ridiculous. When I was sixty-five I had pimples." ~ George Burns

Hours fly; Flowers die. New days, New ways Pass by! Love stays. ~ Henry Van Dyke (from *Katrina's Sun-Dial*)

You may delay, but time will not.[341] ~ Benjamin Franklin

Time is what we want most but what we use worst.[342]
~ William Penn

The future is something which everyone reaches at the rate of sixty minutes an hour, whatever he does, whoever he is.[343]
~ C. S. Lewis

The best use of life is love. The best expression of love is time. The best time to love is now.[344] ~ Rick Warren

There are two days in my calendar: This day and that Day.
~ Martin Luther

Time is the coin of your life. It is the only coin you have, and only you can determine how it will be spent. Be careful lest you let other people spend it for you.[345] ~ Carl Sandburg

It is not that we have so little time but that we lose so much....The life we receive is not short, but we make it so; we are not ill provided but use what we have wastefully. ~ Seneca, On the Shortness of Life

Lost, yesterday, somewhere between sunrise and sunset, two golden hours, each set with sixty diamond minutes. No reward is offered for they are gone forever.[346] ~ Horace Mann

26

Life's Time Clock Is Ticking

Here is a time clock, a mathematical parallel of the seventy-year lifespan with a twenty-four-hour day. Though we are not promised that we will live to this age expectancy or beyond, this life clock gives a visual to help us see how much time has elapsed in life and the potential time that remains to invest in service for God. It is mind-boggling but instructional to realize that a sixty-five-year-old is aging 125 times faster than a twelve-year-old.[347] That being said, I now feel much older!

- —If you are 15, it's 8:51 a.m.
- —If you are 20, it's 11:08 a.m.
- —If you are 25, it's 12:25 p.m.
- —If you are 30, it's 1:25 p.m.
- —If you are 35, it's 2:59 p.m.
- —If you are 40, it's 4:16 p.m.
- —If you are 45, it's 5:43 p.m.
- —If you are 50, it's 6:50 p.m.
- —If you are 55, it's 8:08 p.m.
- —If you are 60, it's 10:11 p.m.
- —If you are 70, it's approaching midnight!

What time is it by this time clock for you? A later time should certainly incite a greater effort in Christian service. Paul gives excellent advice, "This is all the more urgent, for you know how late it is; time is running out. Wake up, for our salvation is nearer now than when we first believed" (Romans 13:11 NLT).

Longevity, according to Dan Buettner, is determined ten percent by genes and ninety percent by lifestyle[348] (not taking into consideration God's timetable). Others suggest the figure is closer to twenty-five percent.

Aging Honorably and Happily

Just for laughs

Harry's wife and doctor insisted he start exercising, so to the gym he went. Following consultation with the trainer, fifty-year-old Harry chose to try out a steep treadmill. The trainer said, "I'm going to set it for ten minutes; if you want to go longer, just press start again." Harry began getting tired after five seconds, and after a minute he jumped off gasping for breath. Looking for a place to sit down, he saw a friend.

"Man," said Harry, "I could barely last a full minute on that treadmill."

"All right, all right," said his buddy, "no reason to brag!"[349]

An African-American pastor failed to show up at his church to preach. The deacons were perplexed, having no idea where he was until someone shared they saw him working at the funeral home. Immediately they departed to the funeral home and asked him why he left the church to be an undertaker. He said "I got tired of preaching to get you straightened out only to see you go back to doing wrong. As an undertaker, once I get you straightened out, you will stay straightened out."

~ The End ~

As an end has now come to this book, just so an end to the book of life will come for all. As seniors, we are now writing that book's final chapter. Just a few more pages, paragraphs or sentences and it will be finished. Write well, my fellow Christian traveler, by using the "ink" of undying faith, uncompromising convic-

Life's Time Clock Is Ticking

tion, unceasing devotion, allegiance, love and service to God, and an unblemished life unto God's glory and honor.

May God give you…

For every storm, a rainbow,
For every tear, a smile,
For every care, a promise,
And a blessing in each trial.

For every problem life sends,
A faithful friend to share,
For every sigh, a sweet song,
And an answer for each prayer. ~ An Irish Prayer

Endnotes

[1] Henry Wadsworth Longfellow, "Autumn Within."

[2] John Godfrey Saxe, *The Poems of John Godfrey Saxe, Complete Ed.* (Boston: Houghton, Mifflin and Company, 1882), 2.

[3] C. H. Spurgeon, "The God of the Aged" (sermon #81). May 25, 1856, at the New Park Street Chapel, Southwark.

[4] Billy Graham, *Nearing Home.* (Nashville: Thomas Nelson, 2011), Introduction.

[55] J. Gordon Harris, *Biblical Perspectives on Aging,* (Second Edition) (New York: The Haworth Press, 2008), 158.

[6] Billy Graham, *Newsweek,* Aug. 14, 2006.

[7] "How to Handle Your Fear." https://www.lwf.org/bible-study/posts/how-to-handle-your-fear-12389, accessed February 14, 2017.

[8] Dick Lincoln, "The Monster Under the Bed" (sermon). February 26, 2017, Shandon Baptist, Columbia, SC.

[9] Chuck Swindoll, *Growing Strong in the Seasons of Life.* (Grand Rapids: Zondervan, 1983), 395.

[10] A Conversation with Elisabeth Elliot, https://www.reviveourhearts.com/radio/ revive-our-hearts/true-heroes-faith, accessed February 13, 2017.

[11] W. Barclay (Ed.), *The Letters to the Corinthians.* (Philadelphia: The Westminster John Knox Press, 1975), 201.

[12] Michael Green, *Illustrations for Biblical Preaching.* (Grand Rapids: Baker Book House, 1991), 148.

[13] J. C. Ryle, *Thoughts for Young Men.* (Charles Nolan Publishing, 2002), 9.

[14] John Wesley, *How to Pray: The Best of John Wesley on Prayer.* (Uhrichsville, Ohio: Barbour Publishing Inc., 2007), 29.

[15] Dallas Theological Seminary podcast. Charles Swindoll, "Finishing Well." December 11, 2012.

[16] W. Wiersbe, *The Wycliffe Handbook of Preaching and Preachers.* 193.

[17] J. Robert Clinton, *The Making of a Leader.* (Colorado Springs, CO: NavPress, 1988).

[18] George Sheehan, *Running and Being.* (Simon and Schuster, 1978), 221.

[19] W. Barclay (Ed.), *The Letters to Timothy, Titus, and Philemon.* (Philadelphia: Westminster John Knox Press, 1975), 210.

[20] Ibid.

[21] Ibid.

[22] M. Henry, *Matthew Henry's Commentary on the Whole Bible: Complete and Unabridged in One Volume.* (Peabody: Hendrickson, 1994), 2319.

[23] Ibid.

[24] Martyn Lloyd-Jones, *The Christian Soldier.* (Grand Rapids: Baker, 1977), 179.

[25] W. Barclay, (Ed.), *The Letters to the Galatians and Ephesians.* (Philadelphia: The Westminster John Knox Press, 1976), 183.

[26] Warren Wiersbe, *The Bible Exposition Commentary, NT Vol. 2.* (Colorado Springs: Victor, 1989), 317.

[27] Andrew Murray. *The New Life: Words of God for Young Disciples of Christ,* 1901. Leopold Classic Library (March 15, 2016), 58.

[28] W. Barclay, (Ed.), *The Letters to the Galatians and Ephesians.* (Philadelphia: The Westminster John Knox Press, 1976), 184.

[29] E. M. Bounds, *Power Through Prayer.* (Cosimo, Inc., 2007), 123.

[30] C. H. Spurgeon, *An All-Around Ministry.* (BiblioBazaar, LLC, 2008), 227.

[31] W. Y. Fullerton, *Charles Haddon Spurgeon: A Biography.* A Triumphant End, Chapter 19. http://www.spurgeon.org/misc/bio19.php, accessed January 18, 2017.

[32] http://www.christianpost.com/news/finishing-well-a-lesson-from-my-grandfather-billy-graham-on-his-95th-birthday-108290/#5VIJXOXSYX2mWCmC. 99. Accessed January 18, 2017.

Endnotes

33 Oswald Chambers, *The Place of Help.* (Discovery House Publishers, December 1989).

34 Harry John Wilmot-Buxton, *The Lord's Song: Plain Sermons on Hymns.* (London: W. Skeffington & Son, 1880), 30.

35 W. A. Criswell. "Give Me This Mountain," (sermon, January 5, 1969). http://www.wacriswell.org/PrintTranscript.cfm/SID/2632.cfm, accessed February 4, 2017.

36 Ella Wheeler Wilcox, *Maurine, and Other Poems.* (Chicago: Belford-Clarke Co., 1890), 145

37 http://vancehavner.com/biography/, accessed October 23, 2016.

38 Henry Durbanville, *The Best Is Yet to Be.* (Edinburgh, Scotland: B. McCall Barbour, 1962), 46.

39 *Lives of the Artists: Michelangelo.* (Milwaukee: Garth Stevens Publishing, 2004). 41–42.

40 http://www.gty.org/resources/sermons/56-13/gods-plan-for-older-men-and-older-women, accessed October 24, 2016.

41 Ralph Winter, "The Retirement Booby Trap," Mission Frontiers 7, (July 1985), 25.

42 Frank Stagg, *The Bible Speaks on Aging.* (Nashville: Broadman Press, 1981), 186.

43 C. H. Spurgeon, "The God of the Aged" (sermon # 81). May 25, 1856, at the New Park Street Chapel, Southwark.

44 Billy Graham, "It's Never Too Late to Be Used by God." http://christiantoday.com.au/news/billy-graham-its-never-too-late-to-be-used-by-god.html, accessed February 25, 2017.

45 https://bible.org/seriespage/psalm-71-growing-old-god%E2%80%99s-way, accessed October 18, 2016.

46 P. L. Tan, *Encyclopedia of 7700 Illustrations: Signs of the Times.* (Garland, TX: Bible Communications, Inc., 1996), 937.

[47] https://www.uab.edu/ullmanmuseum, accessed February 1, 2017.

[48] http://www.thoughts-about-god.com/quotes/quotes-aging.html, accessed February 4, 2017.

[49] Frank Stagg, *The Bible Speaks on Aging.* (Nashville: Broadman Press, 1981), 182.

[50] C. H. Spurgeon. "The God of the Aged," Sermon #81, May 25, 1856. http://www.spurgeon.org/sermons/0081.php, accessed February 15, 2017.

[51] C. H. Spurgeon. "The Remembrance of Christ," sermon delivered January 7, 1855. http://www.spurgeon.org/sermons/0002.php, accessed February 6, 2017.

[52] https://www.christianquotes.info/top-quotes/22-motivating-quotes-about-prayer/#axzz4XwcXBYxu, accessed February 6, 2017.

[53] Ibid.

[54] Fred Barlow. *Evangelist John R. Rice: Giant of Evangelism!* (Murfreesboro, TN: Sword of the Lord Publishers, 1983). www.soulwinning.info/gs/john_rice/giant.htm. accessed April 9, 2010. Author italicized the statement about Rice's hot tears.

[55] https://www.brainyquote.com/quotes/keywords/suffering_9.html, accessed February 7, 2017.

[56] https://www.brainyquote.com/quotes/keywords/suffering_9.html, accessed February 7, 2017.

[57] Frank Stagg, *The Bible Speaks on Aging.* (Nashville: Broadman Press, 1981), 188.

[58] www.short-funny.com, accessed March 27, 2017.

[59] https://www.brainyquote.com/quotes/quotes/c/cslewis151465.html, accessed February 8, 2017.

[60] http://www.biblebaptistliveoak.com/index.cfm?i=11980&mid=1000&id=277637, accessed January 2, 2017.

Endnotes

61 https://www.brainyquote.com/quotes/quotes/e/edwinhubbe157037.html, accessed February 12, 2017.

62 Paul E. Little, *Know What You Believe*. (Wheaton: Victor Books, 1979), 189.

63 Jon Courson, *Jon Courson's Application Commentary*, 556.

64 *The Placed Called Heaven*, Christ for the World Publishers, 1959.

65 Ibid.

66 C. H. Spurgeon, "Landlord and Tenants."

67 C. H. Spurgeon, *Morning and Evening*. (Grand Rapids: Zondervan Publishing House, 1969), January 18.

68 Max Lucado, "Experiencing the Heart of Jesus: Knowing His Heart, Feeling His Love."

69 Billy Graham, *Where I Am: Heaven, Eternity, and Our Life Beyond*. (Nashville: Thomas Nelson, 2015).

70 Ibid.

71 http://www.christianitytoday.com/ct/2011/januaryweb-only/qabillygraham.html, accessed October 24, 2016.

72 Eliza E. Hewitt, cited in William Kirkpatrick and Henry Gilmour, *Pentecostal Praises*. (Philadelphia: Hall-Mack Company, 1898).

73 http://www.short-funny.com/funny-sayings.php#ixzz4cOaJ0BqS, accessed March 27, 2017.

74http://www.goodreads.com/quotes/550900-if-wrinkles-must-be-written-upon-our-brows-let-them, accessed February 12, 2017.

75 Spurgeon, "Light at Evening Time," October 25, 1857, The New Park Street Pulpit, sermon #160.

76 J. Gordon Harris, *Biblical Perspectives on Aging*. (New York: The Hayworth Press, 2008), 39.

77 http://www.goodreads.com/quotes/tag/mentoring?page=, accessed February 15, 2017.

78 Interview with Elizabeth Elliot, https://www.reviveourhearts.com/radio/revive-our-hearts/true-heroes-faith, accessed February 15, 2017.

79http://www.gty.org/resources/sermons/56-13/gods-plan-for-older-men-and-older-women, accessed October 24, 2016.

80 A. W. Pink, *An Exposition of Hebrews.* (Swengel, PA: Bible Truth Depot, 1954), 590.

81 "A Lasting Legacy." June 2015: A Word from Dr. Stanley, www.intouch.org. accessed February 20, 2017.

82 https://www.westernseminary.edu/transformedblog/2012/07/06/aging-biblically, accessed October 18, 2016.

83 http://www.rd.com/jokes/old-age/, accessed October 22, 2016.

84 http://www.elderoptionsoftexas.com/jokes.htm, accessed March 25, 2017.

85 Ibid.

86 http://www.goodreads.com/quotes/tag/growing-old, accessed October 25, 2016.

87 http://purelovequotes.com, accessed February 23, 2017.

88 James Dobson, *What Wives Which Their Husbands Knew About Women.* (Tyndale Momentum, October 1, 1981), http://drjamesdobson.org/blogs/dr-dobson-blog-dr-dobson-blog/2015/08/09/men-women-and-aging, accessed February 25, 2016.

89 Max Lucado, *On the Anvil.* (Wheaton, Illinois: Tyndale House Publishers, 2008), 112.

90 BrainyQuote.com, accessed February 1, 2017.

91 http://www.todayschristianmusic.com/artists/steven-curtis-chapman/features/story-behind-the-song-i-will-be-here, accessed February 3, 2017.

92 Gary Collins, *Family Shock,* 27.

Endnotes

[93] Ibid.

[94] Jeff Anderson. "10 Best Things About Growing Old," Posted 20 Sept. 2016. http://www.aplaceformom.com/blog/best-things-about-growing-old-9-4-13, accessed March 11, 2017.

[95] Amy Goyer. "5 *Don't*s of Grandparenting," November 9, 2010. www.aarp.org/relationships/grandparenting/info.../goyer_grandparenting_advice.html, accessed March 13, 2017.

[96] Prayer and Intercession Quotes. www.tentmaker.org.

[97] http://www.jokes4us.com/peoplejokes/grandpajokes.html, accessed March 11, 2017.

[98] http://www.enkivillage.com/growing-old-together-quotes.html, accessed February 3, 2017.

[99] https://www.brainyquote.com/quotes/quotes/r/robertfros163221.html, February 24, 2017.

[100] http://www.thoughts-about-god.com/quotes/quotes-aging.html, accessed February 4, 2017.

[101] C. H. Spurgeon, "The God of the Aged" (sermon # 81). May 25, 1856, at the New Park Street Chapel, Southwark.

[102] Biblical Illustrator.

[103] http://www.elderoptionsoftexas.com/jokes.htm, accessed March 25, 2017.

[104] https://www.brainyquote.com/quotes/keywords/loneliness.html, accessed February 17, 2017.

[105] https://www.brainyquote.com/quotes/keywords/loneliness_2.html, accessed February 17, 2017.

[106] James C. Dobson, "Life on the Edge: The Next Generation's Guide to a Meaningful Future." https://www.goodreads.com/quotes/7951819-29-most-loneliness-results-from-insulation-rather-than-isolation-in, accessed February 17, 2017.

[107] C. H. Spurgeon, *Morning and Evening*. March 3.

[108] Michael Warden, "The Transformed Heart," (Lulu.com, 2008), 80.

[109] https://www.brainyquote.com/quotes/keywords/solitude.html, accessed February 18, 2017.

[110] Adrian Rogers, "God's Answer to Loneliness," http://www.oneplace.com/ministries/love-worth-finding/read/articles/gods-answer-to-loneliness-9028.html, accessed February 18, 2017.

[111] https://www.brainyquote.com/quotes/quotes/l/lordbyron150314.html, accessed February 25, 2017.

[112] http://www.oneplace.com/ministries/love-worth-finding/read/articles/gods-answer-to-loneliness-9028.html, accessed February 18, 2017.

[113] Ibid.

[114] "Why Did Jesus Cry, 'My God, My God, Why Have You Forsaken Me?,'" https://www.gty.org/library/print/bible-qna/BQ032913, accessed February 18, 2017.

[115] http://www.elderoptionsoftexas.com/jokes.htm, accessed March 25, 2017.

[116] http://biblereasons.com/fear-of-death/, accessed February 28, 2017.

[117] https://www.brainyquote.com/quotes/authors/m/max_lucado.html, assessed January 9, 2017. *And the Angels Were Silent: Walking with Christ toward the Cross.* (2005 edition). (Nashville: Thomas Nelson Inc.).

[118] Sermon 3125. "Fear of Death," December 17, 1874.

[119] T. DeWitt Talmage, "The Ferry Boat of the Jordan" (sermon), http://biblehub.com/sermons/auth/talmage/the_ferry-boat_of_the_jordan.htm, accessed January 2, 2017.

[120] Billy Graham, *Where I Am: Heaven, Eternity, and Our Life Beyond.* (Nashville: Thomas Nelson, 2015).

[121] D. L. Moody, cited in *Funeral Sermons and Outlines.* (Grand Rapids, Michigan: Baker Book House, 1951), 76.

[122] http://www.biblebaptistliveoak.com/index.cfm?i=11980&mid=1000&id=277637, accessed January 2, 2017.

Endnotes

[123] Aubrey Malphurs and Keith Willhite, *A Contemporary Handbook for Weddings and Funerals and Other Occasions.* (Grand Rapids: Kregal Publications, 2006), 238. (adapted)

[124] http://www.christianquotes.info/quotes-by-topic/quotes-about-heaven/?listpage=9&instance=2, accessed January 2, 2017.

[125] Spurgeon, "Landlord and Tenants."

[126] http://www.goodreads.com/quotes/tag/frailty, accessed February 6, 2017.

[127] http://www.bartleby.com/348/44.html, accessed February 12, 2017.

[128] *Our Daily Bread.*

[129] Quoted by C. H. Spurgeon in the sermon "Landlord and Tenants" (No. 3021).

[130] C. H. Spurgeon, "Light at Evening Time." (October 25, 1857).

[131] http://www.elderoptionsoftexas.com/jokes.htm, accessed March 25, 2017.

[132] Max Lucado, *Every Day Deserves a Chance: Wake Up to the Gift of 24 Hours.* (Nashville: Thomas Nelson, 2007).

[133] http://www.goodreads.com/quotes/tag/apology, accessed January 7, 2017.

[134] http://www.goodreads.com/quotes/tag/ingratitude, accessed January 7, 2017.

[135] http://www.azquotes.com/quotes/topics/ingratitude.html, accessed January 7, 2017.

[136] https://www.brainyquote.com/quotes/authors/m/max_lucado.html, accessed January 9, 2017.

[137] Jay E. Adams, *Shepherding God's Flock.* (Grand Rapids: Zondervan, 1974), 136.

[138] Greg Laurie, "Good Grief," http://www.jesus.org/life-of-jesus/teaching-and-messages/good-grief.html, accessed February 19, 2017.

[139] Martha Wickmore Hickman, "Healing After Loss," February 8 entry.

[140] http://www.goodreads.com/quotes/405335-i-think-i-am-beginning-to-understand-why-grief-feels, accessed March 29, 2017.

[141] https://www.google.com/webhp?sourceid=chrome-instant&ion=1&espv=2&ie=UTF-8#q=emily+dickinson&*, accessed March 28, 2017.

[142] *The Life and Death of King John,* Act 3, Scene 4.

[143] Rosane Marazzi, *Lord...Hold My Hand.* (Bloomington, Indiana: WestBow Press, 2013), 49.

[144] Vance Havner, *Hope Thou in God,* 27.

[145] C. S. Lewis, *The Problem of Pain.* (New York: HarperCollins Publishers, 2001), Preface.

[146] C. S. Lewis, *A Grief Observed.* (HarperOne, 2001), 15.

[147] Ibid., 65–66.

[148] "Ruth Bell Graham: A Legacy of Faith." Retrieved 2007-11-15.

[149] "Billy Graham Offers Advice on Growing Old," March 5, 2013. http://blog.christianitytoday.com/ctliveblog/archives/2013/03/billy-graham-offers-advice-on-growing-old.html, accessed April 21, 2013.

[150] Elizabeth Elliot, "Suffering Is Not for Nothing" (a message), *Revive Our Hearts Radio,* March 22, 2013.

[151] Lars Gren. "Ramblings from the Cove," August, 2011. http://www.elisabethelliot.org/ramble/ramblings083111.html, accessed January 11, 2017.

[152] Joyce Rogers, *Grace for the Widow.* (Nashville: B&H Publishing, 2009), Prologue.

[153] Ibid.

[154] Ibid, p. 2.

[155] http://www.charismanews.com/us/41689-after-grieving-wife-s-death-jim-garlow-tells-church-i-m-seeing-someone, accessed January 12, 2017.

[156] W. A. Criswell, "Grief at the Death of Family/Friends," (January 12th, 1958).

Endnotes

[157] Martha Whitmore Hickman, *Healing After Loss: Daily Meditations For Working Through Grief,* (New York: Avon Books, 1994), 9.

[158] Carol Staudacher, *A Time to Grieve.* (New York: HarperCollins Publishers, 1994), 92.

[159] Alexander Allen, *Life and Letters of Phillips Brooks.* (London: McMillian and Company, 1900), 808.

[160] http://www.charismanews.com/us/41689-after-grieving-wife-s-death-jim-garlow-tells-church-i-m-seeing-someone, accessed January 11, 2017.

[161] http://www.growthtrac.com/dealing-with-the-death-of-a-spouse/, accessed January 11, 2017.

[162] Ibid.

[163] Ronald Dunn, *When Heaven Is Silent, Trusting God When Life Hurts.* (Nashville: Thomas Nelson Publishers, 1994).

[164] *Moore Matters*, a publication of Moore College, (Newtown, NSW., Autumn 2011), 13.

[165] Charlie Walton, *When There Are No Words.* (Ventura, California: Pathfinder Publishing, 1999), 50–51.

[166] Ibid, 51.

[167] https://www.scrapbook.com/quotes/doc/8164.html, accessed March 28, 2017.

[168] http://www.christianity.com/church/church-history/timeline/2001-now/the-love-of-charles-and-susannah-spurgeon-11633045.html, accessed January 13, 2017.

[169] http://www.azquotes.com/quote/556671, accessed March 28, 2017.

[170] http://members.tripod.com/~mike_mcqueen/elderly.htm, accessed January 11, 2017.

[171] Erin Prater, "In Sickness and in Health: Tips for Coping with a Diagnosis" (article). http://www.focusonthefamily.com/marriage/facing-crisis/chronic-illness/in-sickness-and-in-health, accessed January 13, 2017.

[172] Hickman, "Healing after Loss," March 4 entry.

[173] http://www.whatchristianswanttoknow.com/21-uplifting-quotes-for-times-of-despair/#ixzz4XwOVe1eF, accessed February 6, 2017.

[174] David Jeremiah. "What Are You Afraid Of?" Book promotional.

[175] https://www.brainyquote.com/quotes/keywords/suffering_4.html, accessed March 27, 2017.

[176] JRSM, v. 94 (11), Nov. 2001.

[177] http://www.webmd.com/sex-relationships/features/chronic-illness-seven-relationship-tips, accessed January 14, 2017.

[178] http://www.focusonthefamily.ca/marriage/midlife-marriage/spousal-caregivers-when-chronic-illness-crashes-into-your-marriage, accessed January 14, 2017.

[179] Ibid.

[180] Ibid.

[181] http://www.webmd.com/sex-relationships/features/chronic-illness-seven-relationship-tips?page=3, accessed January 14, 2017.

[182] Kalb. http://www.webmd.com/sex-relationships/features/chronic-illness-seven-relationship-tips?page=4, accessed January 14, 2017.

[183] Ann Brandt, "In Sickness and in Health." *Mature Living*. (Nashville: Lifeway Press, February, 2017), 49.

[184] www.hopkinsmedicine.org › Health › Healthy Aging › Caregiver Resources, accessed January 14, 2017.

[185] http://www.christianquotes.info/quotes-by-topic/quotes-about-illness/#ixzz4Vfy3nYf3, accessed January 13, 2017.

[186] Preached June 7, 1891.

[187] http://www.christianquotes.info/quotes-by-topic/quotes-about-illness/#ixzz4Vg4C6t6d, accessed January 13, 2017.

Endnotes

[188] https://themighty.com/2015/09/the-impact-of-chronic-illness-on-marriage/, accessed January 14, 2017.

[189] https://foreverfamilies.byu.edu/Pages/marriage/IssuesInMarriage/Coping-with-the-Chronic-Illness-of-a-Spouse.aspx, accessed January 14, 2017.

[190] https://foreverfamilies.byu.edu/Pages/marriage/IssuesInMarriage/Coping-with-the-Chronic-Illness-of-a-Spouse.asp, accessed January 14, 2017.

[191] http://www.webmd.com/sex-relationships/features/chronic-illness-seven-relationship-tips?page=4, accessed January 14, 2017.

[192] Ann Brandt, "In Sickness and In Health."

[193] http://www.focusonthefamily.com/marriage/facing-crisis/chronic-illness/chronic-illness-in-marriage, accessed January 13, 2017.

[194] http://www.webmd.com/sex-relationships/features/chronic-illness-seven-relationship-tips, accessed January 14, 2017.

[195] http://abcnews.go.com/Health/AlzheimersCommunity/pat-robertson-alzheimers-makes-divorce/story?id=14526660, accessed March 24, 2016.

[196] Ashley Willis. "7 Important Things to Do When Your Spouse Is Sick," November 19, 2015. http://sixseeds.patheos.com/ashleywillis/7-important-things-to-do-when-your-spouse-is-sick/, accessed January 14, 2017.

[197] http://www.focusonthefamily.ca/marriage/midlife-marriage/spousal-caregivers-when-chronic-illness-crashes-into-your-marriage, accessed January 14, 2017.

[198] http://members.tripod.com/~mike_mcqueen/elderly.htm, accessed January 11, 2017.

[199] http://www.seniornewways.org/jokes.html, accessed March 25, 2017.

[200] http://www.desiringgod.org/articles/resolutions-on-growing-old-with-god, accessed February 4, 2017.

[201] http://izquotes.com/quote/318656, accessed February 12, 2017.

[202] Frank Stagg, *The Bible Speaks on Aging*. (Nashville: Broadman Press, 1981), 182.

203 "How to Avoid Becoming a Grumpy Old Woman," http://www.healthy women.org/content/article/how-avoid-becoming-grumpy-old-woman, accessed January 16, 2017.

204 Ibid.

205 Sharlta Forrest. "Optimistic People Have Healthier Hearts, Study Finds," Jan. 8, 2015. https://news.illinois.edu/blog/view/6367/204443, accessed January 16, 2017.

206 Ibid.

207 https://www.brainyquote.com/quotes/keywords/optimism.html, accessed January 16, 2017.

208 http://www.goodreads.com/quotes/275720-optimism-hopes-for-the-best-without-any-guarantee-of-its, accessed January 16, 2017.

209 https://billygraham.org/story/9-ways-to-grow-in-your-faith/, accessed January 16, 2017.

210 "How to Avoid Becoming a Grumpy Old Woman." http://www.healthy women.org/content/article/how-avoid-becoming-grumpy-old-woman, accessed January 16, 2017.

211 http://www.livescience.com/35863-grow-old-gracefully-tips.html, accessed March 13, 2017.

212 TheDailyquotes.com, accessed January 16, 2017.

213 Judith Graham. "Older People Become What They Think, Study Shows," (December 19, 2012). https://newoldage.blogs.nytimes.com/2012/12/19/older-people-are-what-they-think-study-shows/?_r=0, accessed January 17, 2017,

214 Ibid.

215 Henry Durbanville, *The Best Is Yet to Be.* (Edinburgh, Scotland: B. McCall Barbour, 1962), 24.

216 Jokes...all from http://members.tripod.com/~mike_mcqueen/elderly.htm, accessed January 17, 2017.

Endnotes

217 https://www.thoughtco.com/golf-one-liners-and-short-funnies-1563919, accessed March 25, 2017.

218 https://twitter.com/davidjeremiah/status/427912875618082817, accessed February 16, 2017.

219 M. Henry, *Matthew Henry's Commentary on the Whole Bible: Complete and Unabridged in One Volume.* (Peabody: Hendrickson, 1994), 1441.

220 Joseph Parker, "The Preacher's Opportunity" (Daniel 5:13–17). http://biblehub.com/commentaries/illustrator/daniel/5.htm, accessed February 13, 2017.

221 http://members.tripod.com/~mike_mcqueen/elderly.htm, accessed February 16, 2017.

222 http://www.smilegodlovesyou.org/jokes.church.html, accessed March 27, 2017.

223 Billy Graham, *Nearing Home,* 19.

224 Interview with Elizabeth Elliot. https://www.reviveourhearts.com/radio/revive-our-hearts/true-heroes-faith, accessed February 19, 2017.

225 Chuck Swindoll. "A Daily Devotional," October 30, 2015.

226 Erskine Neale, *Closing Scene; or Christianity Infidelity Contrasted Last Hours Remarkable Persons.* (London: Longman, Brown, Green and Longmans, 1848), 106.

227 Thought drawn from "Don't Die Before Your Time" by Linda Goldfarb. http://www1.cbn.com/700club/dont-die-your-time, accessed February 16, 2017.

228 Tal D. Bonham and Jack Gulledge, *The Treasury of Clean Senior Adult Jokes* (Broadman) quoted in *Reader's Digest.*

229 http://www.smilegodlovesyou.org/jokes.church.html, accessed March 27, 2017.

230 Charles Rivers, (ed.), *American Legends: The Life of Billy Graham.* (CreateSpace Independent Publishing Platform, June 12, 2015), Introduction.

[231] James Comper Gray, *The Biblical Museum: Old Testament,* Vol. 1. (New York: E. R. Herrick & Co., 1898), 210.

[232] Peter Marshall, *Mr. Jones, Meet the Master: Sermons and Prayers of Peter Marshall.* (Fleming H. Revell Co., 1982), 125.

[233] Adrian Rogers, "Leaving a Legacy" (Sermon Outline). https://www.lwf.org/sermon-outlines/posts/leaving-a-legacy-126, accessed July 12, 2017.

[234] http://www.focusonthefamily.com/parenting/building-relationships/family-legacies/family-legacies-passing-on-a-legacy#, accessed February 21, 2017.

[235] Chuck Swindoll. "A Legacy," *Today's Insight,* October 6, 2016, http://www.crosswalk.com/devotionals/todays-insight-chuck-swindoll/today-s-insight-october-6-2016.html, accessed February 20, 2017.

[236] http://www.focusonthefamily.com/parenting/building-relationships/family-legacies/family-legacies-passing-on-a-legacy#, accessed February 21, 2017.

[237] http://members.tripod.com/~mike_mcqueen/elderly.htm.

[238] http://www.caregiver.com/articles/general/exercise_for_seniors.htm, accessed February 7, 2017. Dr. Montgomery is a family physician, medical epidemiologist and vice-president of Senior Care Solutions with Blue Cross and Blue Shield of Florida.

[239] "The Secrets of Aging Well." http://www.webmd.com/healthy-aging/features/secrets-of-aging-well, accessed February 11, 2017.

[240] *Reader's Digest,* "16 Heart-Health Secrets Cardiologists Want You to Know." http://www.rd.com/health/conditions/13-things-cardiologists-wont-tell-you, accessed February 10, 2017.

[241] Edward Stanley, Earl of Derby (1826-93), British statesman. "The Conduct of Life," address at Liverpool College, 20 Dec 1873.

[242] http://www.caregiver.com/articles/general/exercise_for_seniors.htm, accessed February 7, 2017.

Endnotes

243 http://seniorjournal.com/NEWS/Fitness/2016/20160226_Older-adults-just-need-to-move-a-little-to-extend-life.htm#tM205JWu8oPgfxJH.99, accessed February 7, 2017.

244 The New York Times, February 10, 2017. http://www.nytimes.com/health/guides/specialtopic/physical-activity/exercise's-effects-on-the-heart.html, accessed February 10, 2017.

245 http://seniorjournal.com/NEWS/Fitness/2015/20151124_Another-study-proves-exercise-means-better-memory-for-senior-citizens.htm, accessed February 7, 2017.

246 According to Senior Journal.com cited by Janet Crozier. http://www.caregiver.com/articles/general/exercise_for_seniors.htm, accessed February 7, 2017.

247 SeniorJournal. com.

248 http://seniorjournal.com/NEWS/Fitness/2014/20140828_Fitness_Clearly_a_Fountain_of_Youth.htm, accessed February 7, 2017.

249 NIH SeniorHealth. https://nihseniorhealth.gov/exerciseforolderadults/healthbenefits/01.html, accessed February 8, 2017.

250 http://www.mayoclinic.org/healthy-lifestyle/fitness/multimedia/balance-exercises/sls-20076853, accessed February 7, 2017.

251 Sharon Tanenbaum, "Increase Your Flexibility and Improve Your Life." http://www.realsimple.com/health/fitness-exercise/stretching-yoga/increase-flexibility-improve-life, accessed February 8, 2017.

252 Ibid.

253 Ibid.

254 "5 Ways Exercise Improves Your Quality of Life." http://www.health.harvard.edu/healthbeat/exercise-advice-for-people-with-heart-problems, accessed February 7, 2017.

255 HelpGuide.org. https://www.helpguide.org/articles/exercise-fitness/exercise-and-fitness-as-you-age.htm?pdf=true, accessed February 9, 2017.

[256] "Lots of Seniors Are Overweight, but Few Use Free Counseling For It." http://www.npr.org/sections/health-shots/2015/02/23/387529382/lots-of-seniors-are-overweight-but-few-use-free-counseling, accessed February 9, 2017.

[257] *Reader's Digest,* "30 Things Heart Doctors Do to Protect Their Own Hearts." http://www.rd.com/health/conditions/heart-doctors-heart-health, accessed February 10, 2017.

[258] https://sleepfoundation.org/sleep-news/study-physical-activity-impacts-overall-quality-sleep, accessed February 7, 2017.

[259] http://www.caregiver.com/articles/general/exercise_for_seniors2.htm, accessed February 7, 2017.

[260] The MayoClinic.org, http://www.mayoclinic.org/healthy-lifestyle/nutrition-and-healthy-eating/in-depth/art-20044256?pg=1, accessed February 11, 2017.

[261] http://www.mayoclinic.org/healthy-lifestyle/nutrition-and-healthy-eating/in-depth/art-20044256?pg=1, accessed February 11, 2017.

[262] Ibid.

[263] R. Morgan Griffin, "Myths About Exercise and Older Adults." http://www.webmd.com/healthy-aging/nutrition-world-2/exercise-older-adults?page=1, accessed February 8, 2017.

[264] Ibid.

[265] Ibid.

[266] Ibid.

[267] Ibid.

[268] http://aginginstride.enewsworks.com/en/10022/articles/915/Five-Myths-About-Exercise-and-Healthy-Aging.htm#sthash.BCbY3vho.dpuf, accessed February 9, 2017.

[269] Ibid.

[270] "The Secrets of Aging Well." http://www.webmd.com/healthy-aging/features/secrets-of-aging-well, accessed February 11, 2017.

Endnotes

271 http://www.short-funny.com/funniest-jokes-9.php#ixzz4cOY4TWge, accessed March 27, 2017.

272 Henry W. Longfellow, *Morituri Salutamus.*

273 C. H. Spurgeon, "Light at Evening Time," October 25, 1857, The New Park Street Pulpit, sermon # 160.

274 Professor Karl Pillemer of Cornell University. "Priceless Advice from Older Americans," http://www.aplaceformom.com/blog/priceless-advice-from-older-americans, accessed March 13, 2017.

275 http://www.goodreads.com/quotes/tag/time, accessed April 15, 2017.

276 C. H. Spurgeon. "The God of the Aged," (sermon # 81). May 25, 1856 at the New Park Street Chapel, Southwark.

277 "Getting Old for the Glory of God," http://www.desiringgod.org/messages/getting-old-for-the-glory-of-god, accessed February 14, 2017.

278 Charles Cowman. *Streams in the Desert,* September 27 entry.

279 Charles Yrigoyen, *John Wesley: Holiness of Heart and Life,* and P. L. Tan, *Encyclopedia of 7700 Illustrations: Signs of the Times.* (Garland, TX: Bible Communications, Inc., 1996), 933–934.

280 Henry Durbanville, *The Best Is Yet to Be.* (Edinburgh, Scotland: B. McCall Barbour, 1962).

281 Ibid.

282 J. C. Ferdinand Pittman, *Bible Truths Illustrated.* (Cincinnati: The Standard Publishing Company, 1917), 293.

283 http://www.thoughts-about-god.com/quotes/quotes-aging.html, accessed February 4, 2017.

284 P. L. Tan, *Encyclopedia of 7700 Illustrations: Signs of the Times.* (Garland, TX: Bible Communications, Inc., 1996), 936.

285 Chuck Swindoll, "Growing Old," *A Daily Devotional,* October 30, 2015.

286 Max Lucado, "Abundant Life," *Lucado Devotional Bible, NCV.*

[287] Sarah Pulliam Bailey, interview with Billy Graham. "Q & A: Billy Graham on Aging, Regrets, and Evangelicals." http://www.christianitytoday.com/ct/2011/januaryweb-only/qabillygraham.html, accessed February 16, 2017.

[288] https://www.gty.org/library/sermons-library/56-13/gods-plan-for-older-men-and-older-women, accessed February 16, 2017.

[289] Richard L. Morgan, Howard Morgan, John C. Morgan, (Ed.), *In the Shadow of Grace: The Life and Meditations of G. Campbell Morgan*. (Eugene, Oregon: Wipf and Stock Publishers, 2009), 103.

[290] W. Somerset Maugham, "The Summing Up."

[291] http://www.cslewis.org/aboutus/faq/quotes-misattributed/

[292] http://www.thoughts-about-god.com/quotes/quotes-aging.html, accessed February 4, 2017.

[293] http://www.goodreads.com/quotes/tag/age, accessed February 23, 2017.

[294] Hickman, *Healing After Loss,* Introduction.

[295] Albert B. Paine, *Mark Twain's Letters.* (New York and London: Harper & Brothers Publishers, 1917), 709.

[296] Cited by Chuck Swindoll, https://www.insight.org/resources/article-library/individual/creating-a-legacy-preparing-the-stones, accessed February 19, 2017.

[297] *The Westminster* (Vol. 32). (April 6, 1907), 7.

[298] Ted Goodman, (ed.), *Forbes' Book of Quotations.*

[299] W. Somerset Maugham, *The Summing Up.* (1938), 290.

[300] Henry Ward Beecher, "Life Thoughts."

[301] Robert Browning, "The Flight of the Duchess."

[302] *Theodore Roosevelt on Bravery: Lessons from the Most Courageous Leader of the Twentieth Century.*

[303] Thomas Jefferson, letter to Francis Adrian Van Der Kemp, January 11, 1825.

Endnotes

[304] Charles Noel Douglas, *Forty Thousand Quotations, Prose and Poetical.* (London: George G. Harrap & Co. LTD, 1917), 51.

[305] Joseph Demakis, *The Ultimate Book of Quotations.* (Raleigh, NC: Lulu Enterprises, Inc., 2012), 4.

[306] http://www.quoteland.com/author/Lord-Chesterfield-Quotes/723, accessed February 12, 2017.

[307] Eleanor Roosevelt, *Book of Common Sense Etiquette.*

[308] William Wordsworth, *The Fountain (Complete Poetical Works),* (1888).

[309] http://www.thoughts-about-god.com/quotes/quotes-aging.html, accessed February 4, 2017.

[310] BrainyQuote.com, accessed February 1, 2017.

[311] J. C. Ryle. *Coming Events and Present Duties Being Plain Papers on Prophecy,* October 1879, Preface.

[312] http://www.bartleby.com/348/44.html, accessed February 12, 2017.

[313] C. H. Spurgeon, "At Evening Time It Shall Be Light," October 25, 1857.

[314] Ibid.

[315] Chambers, "The Place of Help," 1032L.

[316] T. S. Elliot, *The Four Quartets.* (New York: Houghton Mifflin Harcourt Publishing Company, 1971), 16.

[317] http://www.livescience.com/35863-grow-old-gracefully-tips.html, accessed March 13, 2017.

[318] https://www.helpguide.org/articles/emotional-health/laughter-is-the-best-medicine.htm, accessed March 13, 2017.

[319] "5 Radical Life Lessons I Learned from People over 80." http://www.mind bodygreen.com/0-24616/5-radical-life-lessons-i-learned-from-people-over-80.html, accessed March 14, 2017.

[320] Ibid.

[321] Ibid.

[322] Ibid.

[323] Ibid.

[324] "Six Life Lessons I've Learned While Visiting the Elderly." http://www.the mindwell.com/home/six-life-lessons-ive-learned-while-visiting-the-elderly, accessed March 14, 2017.

[325] "100 Pieces of Advice from 100-Year-Olds." http://mentalfloss.com/ article/54286/100-pieces-advice-100-year-olds, accessed March 14, 2017.

[326] Ibid.

[327] Ibid.

[328] Ibid.

[329] Ibid.

[330] Ibid.

[331] Ibid.

[332] Ibid.

[333] Ibid.

[334] Ibid.

[335] Susie Moore, "The 5 Biggest Regrets People Have Before They Die." http://greatist.com/live/most-common-regrets, accessed March 14, 2017.

[336] Phillip Freeman. "10 lessons on Aging and Retirement That Have Lasted 2,050 Years." Based on Cicero. www.marketwatch.com, accessed March 16, 2017.

[337] Angela Mollard, "8 Life Lessons Old People Can Teach Us" (March 1, 2015). http://www.news.com.au, accessed March 16, 2017.

[338] Henry Durbanville, *The Best Is Yet to Be*. (Edinburgh, Scotland: B. McCall Barbour, 1962), 23.

[339] Ibid.

Endnotes

[340] http://thinkexist.com/quotations/elderly/3.html, accessed March 14, 2017.

[341] http://www.goodreads.com/quotes/tag/time, accessed April 15, 2017.

[342] Ibid.

[343] Ibid.

[344] Ibid.

[345] Ibid.

[346] Ibid.

[347] Dan Buettner, "How to Live to Be 100+" (video). https://www.ted.com/playlists/227/talks_to_make_you_feel_good_ab, accessed March 16, 2017.

[348] Ibid.

[349] http://www.greatcleanjokes.com/jokes/senior-jokes/, accessed March 15, 2017.

CPSIA information can be obtained
at www.ICGtesting.com
Printed in the USA
JSHW020557140422
24904JS00005B/68